Shakespeare and Posthumanist Theory

ARDEN SHAKESPEARE AND THEORY

Series Editor: Evelyn Gajowski

AVAILABLE TITLES

Shakespeare and Cultural Materialist Theory
Christopher Marlow
Shakespeare and Economic Theory David Hawkes
Shakespeare and Ecocritical Theory Gabriel Egan
Shakespeare and Ecofeminist Theory Rebecca Laroche
and Jennifer Munroe
Shakespeare and Feminist Theory Marianne Novy
Shakespeare and New Historicist Theory Neema Parvini
Shakespeare and Postcolonial Theory Jyotsna G. Singh
Shakespeare and Psychoanalytic Theory Carolyn Brown
Shakespeare and Queer Theory Melissa E. Sanchez

FORTHCOMING TITLES

Shakespeare and Adaptation Theory Sujata Iyengar
Shakespeare and Performance History David McCandless
Shakespeare and Presentist Theory Evelyn Gajowski
Shakespeare and Race Theory Arthur L. Little, Jr
Shakespeare and Reception Theory Nigel Wood
Shakespeare and Textual History Suzanne Gossett

Shakespeare and Posthumanist Theory

Karen Raber

THE ARDEN SHAKESPEARE
LONDON • NEW YORK • OXFORD • NEW DELHI • SYDNEY

THE ARDEN SHAKESPEARE
Bloomsbury Publishing Plc
50 Bedford Square, London, WC1B 3DP, UK
1385 Broadway, New York, NY 10018, USA

BLOOMSBURY, THE ARDEN SHAKESPEARE and the Arden Shakespeare logo are trademarks of Bloomsbury Publishing Plc

First published in Great Britain 2018
This paperback edition published 2020

Copyright © Karen Raber, 2018, 2020

Karen Raber has asserted her right under the Copyright, Designs and Patents Act, 1988, to be identified as author of this work.

For legal purposes the Acknowledgements on pp. x–xi constitute an extension of this copyright page.

Series design by Sutchinda Rangsi Thompson
Cover image: X-ray of the star turban shell © Surfactant/Getty Images

All rights reserved. No part of this publication may be reproduced or transmitted in any form or by any means, electronic or mechanical, including photocopying, recording, or any information storage or retrieval system, without prior permission in writing from the publishers.

Bloomsbury Publishing Plc does not have any control over, or responsibility for, any third-party websites referred to or in this book. All internet addresses given in this book were correct at the time of going to press. The author and publisher regret any inconvenience caused if addresses have changed or sites have ceased to exist, but can accept no responsibility for any such changes.

A catalogue record for this book is available from the British Library.

Library of Congress Cataloging-in-Publication Data
Names: Raber, Karen, 1961- author.
Title: Shakespeare and posthumanist theory/Karen Raber.
Description: London; New York: Bloomsbury Arden Shakespeare, 2018. | Includes bibliographical references and index.
Identifiers: LCCN 2017043796 (print) | LCCN 2017045088 (ebook) | ISBN 9781474234467 (epdf) | ISBN 9781474234450 (epub) | ISBN 9781474234436 (hardback: alk. paper) | ISBN 9781474234443 (pbk.: alk. paper)
Subjects: LCSH: Shakespeare, William, 1564-1616–Criticism and interpretation. | Humanism in literature. | Philosophical anthropology in literature. | Human body (Philosophy)
Classification: LCC PR3001 (ebook) | LCC PR3001.R33 2018 (print) | DDC 822.3/3–dc23
LC record available at https://lccn.loc.gov/2017043796

ISBN:	HB:	978-1-474-23443-6
	PB:	978-1-4742-3444-3
	ePDF:	978-1-474-23446-7
	eBook:	978-1-474-23445-0

Series: Shakespeare and Theory

Typeset by Integra Software Services Pvt. Ltd.

To find out more about our authors and books visit www.bloomsbury.com and sign up for our newsletters.

CONTENTS

List of Figures vi
Series Editor's Preface vii
Acknowledgements x

1 We Have Never Been Humanist: Genealogies of Posthumanism 1

2 Posthuman Cosmography 27

3 Bodies and Minds 55

4 Neither Fish nor Fowl 89

5 Techno-Bard 125

6 Post-posthumanism? Back to the Future 159

Appendix 166
Notes 168
Bibliography 182
Index 195

LIST OF FIGURES

5.1 Giuseppe Arcimboldo, *Vertumnus* (Emperor Rudolf II), 1590. Oil on wood, 70.5 × 57.5 cm. Courtesy of Art Resource   127

5.2 Giuseppe Arcimboldo, *The Librarian*, 1566. Oil on canvas, 97 × 71 cm. Courtesy of Art Resource   128

5.3 Albrecht Dürer, 'Stereometric Man'. Courtesy of the Saxon State and University Library, Dresden (SLUB Dresden / Digitale Sammlungen / S.B.6023)   140

5.4 Giovanni Bracelli, *Bizarre Figures*, 1624 (etching). The Israel Museum, Jerusalem, Israel. Vera & Arturo Schwarz Collection of Dada and Surrealist Art, courtesy of Bridgeman Images   143

5.5 Giovanni Bracelli, *Bizarre Figures*, 1624 (etching). The Israel Museum, Jerusalem, Israel. Vera & Arturo Schwarz Collection of Dada and Surrealist Art, courtesy of Bridgeman Images   144

SERIES EDITOR'S PREFACE

'Asking questions about literary texts – that's literary criticism. Asking "Which questions shall we ask about literary texts?" – that's literary theory'. So goes my explanation of the current state of English studies, and Shakespeare studies, in my never-ending attempt to demystify, and simplify, theory for students in my classrooms. Another way to put it is that theory is a systematic account of the nature of literature, the act of writing and the act of reading.

One of the primary responsibilities of any academic discipline – whether in the natural sciences, the social sciences or the humanities – is to examine its methodologies and tools of analysis. Particularly at a time of great theoretical ferment, such as that which has characterized English studies, and Shakespeare studies, in recent years, it is incumbent upon scholars in a given discipline to provide such reflection and analysis. We all construct meanings in Shakespeare's texts and culture. Shouldering responsibility for our active role in constructing meanings in literary texts, moreover, constitutes a theoretical stance. To the extent that we examine our own critical premises and operations, that theoretical stance requires reflection on our part. It requires honesty, as well. It is thereby a fundamentally radical act. All critical analysis puts into practice a particular set of theoretical premises. Theory occurs from a particular standpoint. There is no critical practice that is somehow devoid of theory. There is no critical practice that is not implicated in theory. A common-sense, transparent encounter with any text is thereby impossible. Indeed, to the extent that theory requires us to question anew that with which we thought we were familiar, that which we thought we understood, theory constitutes a critique of common sense.

Since the advent of postmodernism, the discipline of English studies has undergone a seismic shift. And the discipline of Shakespeare studies has been at the epicentre of this shift. Indeed, it has been Shakespeare scholars who have played a major role in several of the theoretical and critical developments (e.g. new historicism, cultural materialism, presentism) that have shaped the discipline of English studies in recent years. Yet a comprehensive scholarly analysis of these crucial developments has yet to be done, and is long overdue. As the first series to foreground analysis of contemporary theoretical developments in the discipline of Shakespeare studies, *Arden Shakespeare and Theory* aims to fill a yawning gap.

To the delight of some and the chagrin of others, since 1980 or so, theory has dominated Shakespeare studies. *Arden Shakespeare and Theory* focuses on the state of the art at the outset of the twenty-first century. For the first time, it provides a comprehensive analysis of the theoretical developments that are emerging at the present moment, as well as those that are dominant or residual in Shakespeare studies.

Each volume in the series aims to offer the reader the following components: to provide a clear definition of a particular theory; to explain its key concepts; to trace its major developments, theorists and critics; to perform a reading of a Shakespeare text; to elucidate a specific theory's intersection with or relationship to other theories; to situate it in the context of contemporary political, social and economic developments; to analyse its significance in Shakespeare studies; and to suggest resources for further investigation. Authors of individual volumes thereby attempt to strike a balance, bringing their unique expertise, experience and perspectives to bear upon particular theories while simultaneously fulfilling the common purpose of the series. Individual volumes in the series are devoted to elucidating particular theoretical perspectives, such as adaptation, cultural materialism, ecocriticism, ecofeminism, economic theory, feminism, film theory, new historicism, postcolonialism, posthumanism, presentism, psychoanalysis, queer theory, and race theory.

Arden Shakespeare and Theory aims to enable scholars, teachers and students alike to define their own theoretical strategies and refine their own critical practices. And students have as much at stake in these theoretical and critical enterprises – in the reading and the writing practices that characterize our discipline – as do scholars and teachers. Janus-like, the series looks forward as well as backward, serving as an inspiration and a guide for new work in Shakespeare studies at the outset of the twenty-first century, on the one hand, and providing a retrospective analysis of the intellectual labour that has been accomplished in recent years, on the other.

To return to the beginning: What is at stake in our reading of literary texts? Once we come to understand the various ways in which theory resonates with not only Shakespeare's texts, and literary texts, but the so-called 'real' world – the world outside the world of the mind, the world outside the world of academia – then we come to understand that theory is capable of powerfully enriching not only our reading of Shakespeare's texts, and literary texts, but our lives.

* * *

I am indebted to David Avital, publisher at Bloomsbury Academic, who was instrumental in developing the idea of the *Arden Shakespeare and Theory* series. I am also grateful to Margaret Bartley and Mark Dudgeon, publishers for the Arden Shakespeare, for their guidance and support throughout the development of this series.

Evelyn Gajowski
Series Editor
University of Nevada, Las Vegas

ACKNOWLEDGEMENTS

First, I'd like to thank Evelyn Gajowski for offering me the opportunity to contribute this volume to the *Arden Shakespeare and Theory* series, and I thank her and Dorothy Vanderford for their helpful comments on a draft of the project. Thanks also to Debapriya Sarkar for her responses to a version of Chapter 2. Several portions of the book were first circulated at conferences where they were given receptive readings and helpful comments by Jennifer Munroe, Amy Tigner, Rebecca Laroche, Keith Botelho, Jeffrey Jerome Cohen, Vin Nardizzi, Alicia Pederson, Shannon Kelley and Claire Dawkins. I am lucky enough to have been able to see colleagues' work in progress that gave me a sense of developing areas in posthumanist theory and Shakespeare studies: two deserve special mention, Ben Bertram and Rebecca Totaro, who are publishing monographs in the series I edit for Routledge, Perspectives on the Non-Human in Literature and Culture. My wonderful graduate students who have been enrolled in seminars over the last several years have helped me explore the non-human world of early modernity, especially Nathan Likert, whose seminar and thesis work on the materiality of voice are cited in Chapter 2. Will Palmer, Eric Delp, Will Mackenzie, Cullen Brown, Andrew Freiman and Sarah Huddleston all valiantly wrestled with theory in my Spring 2017 seminar, during which I essentially taught this book: my thanks to them for joining me in the process of spinning up some of the ideas and arguments that appear here. Ivo Kamps secured a teaching reduction for me at the University of Mississippi in the Fall of 2015 to allow me to focus on this project, for which I am eternally grateful. And as always, I thank all the non-human creatures who have shaped my life and made it so much richer, and whose presence is integral to my writing process: Titus, who is the exact opposite of Shakespeare's fictional character; Spike, Loki, Lily, Mouse, Silvester, Shark; and now Max, who makes an excellent Temple Guard Cat – thank you all for your love and companionship. Finally, Doug McPherson is the glue that holds this assemblage together and makes it all worthwhile.

1

We Have Never Been Humanist: Genealogies of Posthumanism

Bruno Latour's 1993 *We Have Never Been Modern* analyses the 'modern constitution' (the set of principles and beliefs on which the whole premise of modernity is based) bequeathed to us by figures like Robert Boyle and Thomas Hobbes who began the process of purification that we have come to assume defines 'modernity'. The effect of that unwritten constitution is to create a perceived abyss between science and the social, or nature and culture, by scrupulously policing the boundaries between domains and forbidding them from mixing. The confusion of categories is branded as archaic, part of the bad old days before we became modern. But, as Latour argues, these category boundaries and binaries are and have always been a fiction: the same coproduction of nature and culture that characterized premodern thought continued after Boyle and Hobbes as well, throughout the Enlightenment and well into the twentieth century. It was merely obscured by the constitution's imposed blindness: we tell ourselves that we have overcome the messy and unsystematic superstitions of the past, and that science, technology and the human or social sciences have been liberated from the 'bondage' of religion, myth and magic; they have been elevated and rationalized for the betterment of humanity. Latour points out that the costs of enforcing that illusion of freedom, however, have been incalculable, involving 'irreparable crimes' against the natural and cultural worlds, as well as against the self (125).

Yet Latour also warns that absolute and totalizing positions *against* this modernity are as dangerously exceptionalist as the case for it ever was. Rather than a stance of anti-humanism or anti-modernity, what is required to effect change is a thorough reconsideration of the category that undergirds all other categorization: 'before we can amend the constitution', Latour writes, 'we must *relocate the human*' (136, italics added). That does not involve eradicating or exterminating 'the human', since to do so would be to fall back on the mistaken assumption that 'the human' ever existed in the first place, and that it could therefore act as a counter or pole against which the 'non-human' could be constituted. Polarization is anathema in Latour's schema. Neither, therefore, does he abandon the idea of a constitution altogether, but rewrites it to include what it has traditionally excluded, arriving at the idea of a 'parliament of things' that can accommodate human and non-human, entities and systems, who can all converge to discuss 'the object-discourse-nature-society whose new properties astound us all and whose network extends from my refrigerator to the Antarctic by way of chemistry, law, the State, the economy, and satellites' (144). This radically re-imagined constitution might allow us to better navigate an exponentially more complex set of social and environmental challenges.

Posthumanist theory attempts in many forms and with many tools to advance the relocation of the human Latour's argument requires. How that relocation is imagined to be best effected depends in part on whether the price of being 'modern' is estimated as environmental destruction, social and economic oppression, species exploitation and extinction, individual suffering, or some combination of these and other harms, all of which are targeted by different versions of posthumanist theory. Cary Wolfe's book-length exploration of the theory, *What is Posthumanism?* (2010), begins by noting that while there are relatively stable definitions of 'humanism' that you can find through a simple web search, any definition of posthumanism one might turn up is much more contested territory. In its simplest form, posthumanism opposes humanist ideals like belief in the perfectibility of man, assumptions about the universality of morality, the investment in an imperial human will that can ameliorate evil and suffering, and faith in the supremacy of reason over emotion. Its first mention as part of a critical apparatus is usually credited to Ihab Hassan, who locates it as the inevitable culmination of Western metaphysics (1977); yet its full emergence in theory required the many collisions between and among metaphysics and culture that characterized the decades from the 1960s through the early 2000s. Posthumanism, in Rosi Braidotti's account, inherited the deconstruction of Man from the anti-humanist theories of the 1960s and 1970s – Marxism, feminism, post-structuralism and postcolonialism interrogated humanism's premises (2013: 16–25).[1] Human beings were repositioned as products of discourse, of history, of economic and political systems or institutions. Yet these theories were not yet posthumanist in the sense that, as Latour suggests, their assaults on the fortress could often come from or end up in the same place as humanism itself. In some cases, theory shifted boundaries to include previously excluded others in the coveted category, in others it described operations of rhetoric and language without necessarily dislodging the manner in which these produced the human. Decentring versions of white, male, European, Christian, property-owning 'Man' was thus the goal of anti-humanists, but often only in the interests of a more powerful or widely applied version of humanity. Posthumanism instead requires a sea-change, a radical revision of the nature and purpose of the category of the human and of the discourses that constitute it. Wolfe cautions that 'the nature of thought itself must change if it is to be posthumanist':

> [W]hen we talk about posthumanism, we are not just talking about a thematics of the decentering of the human in relation to either evolutionary, ecological, or technological

coordinates (though that is where the conversation usually begins and, all too often, ends); rather, I will insist that we are also talking about *how* thinking confronts that thematics, what thought has to become in the face of those challenges. (2010: xvi)

Posthumanism is thus not only about outcomes, but about starting points, about systems of thought and their methodological implications.

In the next section of this chapter I look at a few of the various origin stories we can tell about posthumanism; I also discuss the permutations that can be grouped under the umbrella of posthumanist theory, and assess what each offers, or fails to offer, a new praxis. I turn then to the problem of bringing posthumanist theory to bear on Shakespeare's work. Latour's deployment of Boyle and Hobbes establishes a fairly recognizable timeline, one in which there is a turn at the start of the Enlightenment that places the Renaissance in the 'before' of some great new historical or ideological phase. Where posthumanism is concerned, claiming it for Shakespeare, or Shakespeare for it, might at first blush therefore seem counterintuitive – surely the Renaissance is precisely humanism's grand moment, witnessing the birth of the reasoning agent, that paragon of creation that posthumanism dismantles. Indeed, Braidotti uses Leonardo da Vinci's Vitruvian Man as her chosen humanist punching bag: this 'standard of both perfection and perfectibility ... was literally pulled down from his pedestal and deconstructed' first by antihumanist theory and later more complexly and completely by posthumanism (2013: 23). Yet the humanism of Shakespeare's world was not the humanism of the Enlightenment, and not entirely the premodern bondage machine that moderns might have imagined it to be. Nor was Renaissance humanism quite as confident of man's perfectibility as Braidotti supposes – or even confident that it knew what a 'man' was in the first place. Indeed, after thinking through Renaissance humanism's reflections and influences on Shakespeare's work, it is entirely possible to conclude that we have never quite, to adapt Latour's endlessly malleable formulation, been humanist. On the one hand, humanism failed to completely unseat medieval thought in medicine, science, theology or politics;[2] on the other, the paradigms it generated did not resolve to a simple set of precepts about human nature or human status in the cosmos. Nor were the humanisms of Erasmus, Pico della Mirandola, Michel de Montaigne or Thomas More identical with one another. Salient figures who benefited from a humanist education and even advocated for what might to us seem like humanist principles do not end up espousing precisely humanist sentiments: for instance, is Milton a humanist? His idiosyncratic theology and late turn against syncretic reading of classical texts make that a difficult question to answer. How about Giambattista Vico, who is called a humanist and appropriated as both a pro- and an anti-Enlightenment thinker, and whose work is credited with influencing figures like Karl Marx and Hayden White? Certainly Vico's anti-Cartesian endorsement of rhetoric and the humanities aligns with traditional Renaissance humanism; yet it is difficult to contain Vico's thought under such a narrow banner. And is post-Cartesian or Enlightenment 'humanism' unproblematically continuous with Renaissance humanism? Twentieth-century theorist Michel Foucault thought not, suggesting that the Enlightenment would have been sceptical of the continued presence of religious elements in earlier humanist thought (see Wolfe 2010: xvi). Yet this perceived distinction sounds subtly like the 'modern constitution' Latour outlines: were we good enough practitioners of Enlightenment scepticism, we could, by applying its principles more rigorously, purge the 'anthropological, political, and scientific dogmas of the human' (Wolfe 2010: xvi). Moreover, as Joe Campana and Scott Maisano point out, posthumanist theorists 'have largely conflated and confused Renaissance and Enlightenment humanisms so that a singular "humanism" has become almost synonymous with "modernity"' (2016: 4). If that is true, what difference might it make to posthumanist practice if historical transpositions and elisions are redressed? We can't answer such questions or address such problems without excavating the myriad strains and histories of what we too-loosely brand 'humanism'.

And finally, the question that inspires this project is what is the relevance of Shakespeare and posthumanist theory to one another? How does it benefit either or both to be in conversation? The remainder of this introduction outlines these and more issues, along with a few clarifying contexts that continue to be elaborated in the several chapters of this book.

Lineages

There are at least two ways to think about posthumanist theory: one is to dive deep into the metaphysical tradition that gives rise to posthumanism, the legacy of Western thought especially since Descartes; the other is to broadly, but more superficially, account for the many current critical and scholarly approaches that can amount to a posthumanist practice. In this section I'll be doing a little of both but will tend toward the latter – consider it a kind of topographical map that will let us think about the points where the theory invites intersections or opportunities for Shakespeare studies.

Posthumanism is now a vast topic with its own subfields, web sites, explanatory books, scholarly dissertations, journals, book series, motivated critics and a substantial pop culture presence.[3] Many of the sources one might cite as examples of all of these conflate posthumanism with the posthuman. It is worth beginning with a brief outline of the difference between being 'posthuman' and being a posthumanist, which is central to one of the field's early influential texts. N. Katherine Hayles's groundbreaking 1999 book *How We Became Posthuman* charted the rise of the posthuman as an effect of cybernetics. Reacting to Hans Moravec's 'roboticist's dream' that it will someday soon be possible to download a human consciousness into a computer, Hayles makes a series of discoveries pertaining to the 'posthuman' as it was imagined in the postwar world of technologies associated with the development of Artificial Intelligence (AI) – information and systems theory, cognitive science, virtual reality – as well as in science fiction and popular culture. Her concern is the manner in which this posthuman has 'lost its body', and although 'in many ways the posthuman deconstructs the liberal humanist subject, it thus shares with its predecessor an emphasis on cognition rather than embodiment' (Hayles 1999: 3, 5):

> I understand human and posthuman to be historically specific constructions that emerge from different configurations of embodiment, technology, and culture. My reference point for the human is the tradition of liberal humanism: the posthuman appears when computation rather than possessive individualism is taken as the ground of being, a move that allows the posthuman to be seamlessly articulated with intelligent machines. (Hayles 1999: 34)

The 'liberal humanist' self Hayles refers to is the autonomous, individuated, rational and perfectible subject we have already met; that subject's sense of individualism and the grounds for its extension of will into the world is the natural ownership of itself, a concept C. B. Macpherson traced in the seventeenth-century political theories of John Locke and Thomas Hobbes.[4] The consequences of what Hayles analyses are significant: the posthuman's rejection of the body underwrites fantasies of uncurbed power, immortality and triumph over the very vulnerabilities that connect us to the non-human world.

At times what Hayles describes and reacts to might best be called 'transhumanism' for its idealized vision of a human that is continuing its evolution through technology in ways that allow its transcendence of limitations, whether of body or of mind. There is a degree of overlap and sometimes confusion of these two positions: the posthuman might be thought of as fully absenting the body's current biological state, while transhumanism adapts and readjusts a biological model of evolution so that it encompasses technology. Transhumanism, however, explicitly does not reject Enlightenment thought: in the words of Max More, 'Transhumanism continues to champion the core of the Enlightenment ideas and ideals – rationality and scientific method, individual rights, the possibility and desirability of progress, the overcoming of superstition and authoritarianism, and the search for new forms of governance' (2013: 10). More disputes criticism of transhumanism's perceived utopianism, insisting that rather than a final resting point in the future, transhumanists embrace 'perpetual progress' (14), and he dismisses the charge that transhumanists 'loathe biological bodies', arguing that rather they aim to ameliorate and enhance the body. Nevertheless, as Hayles might point out, the very notion that bodies must be somehow remedied and transformed is part of 'a *systematic devaluation of materiality and embodiment*' (1999: 48).

Hayles writes as an early posthumanist about the nature of the posthuman as it is imagined by science and culture: I specify this in order to clarify that *the posthuman* is not the same or even always directly related to posthuman*ism* and posthumanist *theory*. Posthuman describes a state of being, often associated with technological advances; a posthuman thus may or may not be thought of as human in the traditional sense of that term. Posthuman*ism* (sometimes usefully called critical posthumanism) might best be defined as any position that puts the premises and precepts of humanism into question; posthumanist theory is the codification of thought, particularly Western philosophical thought, which enables that position. It is entirely possible to be a posthumanist theorist and disagree with aspects of the construction of a posthuman identity, as Hayles does.

Hayles's work has been criticized for a degree of universalism, and for too-emphatically extracting the materiality of the body from its discursive construction. Nevertheless, her work provides an important model for combining cognitive science, systems theory and posthumanist implications in the work of anti-humanist philosophers and theorists. Stephan Herbrechter credits her with the 'breakthrough' inspired by the 'storm' brewing in the 1990s, the era in which the consequences of anti-humanism began to show up in literary and cultural theory (2013: 36). Her work attests to the importance for posthumanism of that era of cultural, historical and literary theory, especially the writings of Jacques Derrida and Michel Foucault. Like Wolfe, she credits (as do many others) Foucault's vision of the 'end of man' at the conclusion of *The Order of Things* as an important juncture initiating the posthumanist turn (Hayles 1999: 293 n.5; Wolfe 2010: xii).[5] Derrida's deconstructive methods constitute what Wolfe describes as the work of Enlightenment rationality applied more rigorously to philosophy itself (2010: xx). Neil Badmington concurs, pointing out that 'while the anti-humanists were declaring a departure from the legacy of humanism, Derrida was patiently pointing out the difficulties of making such a break. Precisely because Western philosophy is steeped in humanist assumptions, he observed, the end of Man is bound to be written in the language of Man' (2000: 9).

But what exactly is the (Enlightenment) Western philosophical tradition Derrida and Foucault engage with? The *Meditations on First Philosophy* and the *Discourse on Method* of René Descartes mark a starting point in the seventeenth century. In order to determine what he could ascertain absolutely to be true, Descartes discarded empirical evidence on the premise that the senses could be misleading. Engaging in a form of radical doubt, Descartes put all things in question, and concluded that the only certain knowledge he could have was that he thought – hence, he knew he existed, or in his famous construction, *cogito ergo sum*. The body, in Descartes's estimation, was thus distinct from and less reliable than the mind; moreover, only human beings could be said to be capable of reason – animals, for instance, had bodies, but these functioned mechanically, without access to genuine communicative language, for instance, which was evidence of a rational mind lodged within. Descartes's application of mathematical standards to the treatment of existence and consciousness, his rejection of sensation as the basis of knowledge, and his establishment of reason as the unique defining property of human beings had direct consequences for subsequent Enlightenment thought. For one thing, his influence bifurcated philosophy into two camps: rationalists, who like Descartes saw truth as emerging from reason, and empiricists, who saw truth in the experience or observation of phenomena. Rationalists and empiricists battled throughout the eighteenth century, until Immanuel Kant initiated yet another paradigm shift (in his 1781 *Critique of Pure Reason*) by proposing that the self in fact could know nothing without reference to external objects; Kant believed that only a synthesis of rationalism and empiricism could end the endless debate between the two philosophical poles. By the nineteenth century, Husserl and Heidegger would play out a different yet parallel form of debate between Husserl's view that only the perception of objects and events counts for constituting the real vs. Heidegger's conception of 'being in the world', or the social connection of the subject.

This admittedly extremely reductive potted history of the Western philosophical tradition suggests historical progression where it does not necessarily obtain in present debates about humanism, philosophy, the Enlightenment or posthumanism – that is to say that most of these views, methods or conclusions remain under constant revision and recirculation. They do not go away. Thus, we can find different posthumanist thinkers using familiar but disparate figures from metaphysics and philosophy as catalysts in their work: Nietzsche (Herbrechter 2013), Freud and Marx (Badmington 2000), Heidegger (Hayles 1999) and Hegel (Moeller 2006) all have their entrances and exits, as do so many others. Kant remains a target, as does Descartes. The reason, many would agree, for the persistence of all these voices is not only that humanism's ideas are difficult to dislodge, but that humanism, particularly Enlightenment humanism, has always carried within itself the seeds of posthumanism. Simply by putting 'man' at the centre of inquiry, philosophy ensured that 'man' would be the focus of intense and eventually destabilizing scrutiny. Badmington cites Marx and Engels alongside Freud for 'opening up a space for what would become posthumanism': the project of establishing exactly what the human subject was or could be was at the heart of Marx and Engels's *The German Ideology* (first conceived in 1846), while Freud did a deep dive into the same human subject in the late nineteenth and early twentieth centuries (Badmington 2000: 5, 6–7). Both charted forces like history, the means of production, the unconscious, forces that produced subjects; it was a short step from these insights to Louis Althusser's conclusion that the subject is 'interpellated' by ideology as well as material conditions, or Jacques Lacan's critique of Freud, and thus of the Cartesian *cogito*. Without the centrality of the human being in Enlightenment thought, there is no 'human' to repeatedly put into question. Further, by promising freedom and liberation, Enlightenment thought required results, leading first to the promulgation and increased inclusivity of liberal rights theory, and then inevitably to questions about its roots and functionality when new groups found it did not confer full enfranchisement. Women, racial and sexual 'others', the poor and working class, those brought into the debate via colonial enterprises, among other marginalized groups and individuals, might challenge humanism on the basis of its exclusion of them from the 'same' of the central concept of 'Man' – but even when established as 'human' they did not necessarily find their dilemmas resolved. Antihumanist thinking from the mid-twentieth century forward thus naturally challenged the extension of 'human' rights as an answer in itself. Indeed in the case of the fate of non-human animals, we can see some of this process at work: first, animals suffer exclusion on the basis of their non-humanity (premodern through early twentieth-century attitudes that animals are worth less than humans and so cannot command the same standards of care or respect), followed by limited inclusion on the basis of welfare and narrow 'rights' (the early protection and welfare movements followed by the argument that the only way to guarantee the alleviation of suffering is to endow animals with some rights before the law) and then finally a turn toward scepticism about rights theory altogether when expansion fails to accomplish enough because 'the human' persists as the legitimizing factor in such moves.[6]

Posthumanist thought thus has many progenitors, an uncertain and fluid lineage – and spawns as many offspring as humanism has and still does. Among those offspring I'll be able to cover here only a selection: animal studies, body studies, cognitive ecology, ecocriticism, the new materialisms and ecomaterialism, and systems theory. When I account for these, I am creating a narrative about phenotype, not genotype; some strains of each cooperate with and contribute to or uphold posthumanism, some do not. Yet critical expressions of all of these can resonate with each other and enact the theory's several agendas.

Animal studies, for instance, has recently become a main means for achieving posthumanist insights into literature, history and culture. For Wolfe, Donna Haraway, Giorgio Agamben, Vincianne Despret, Martha Nussbaum, Carole Adams, or Gilles Deleuze and Felix Guattari, deconstructing the category of the animal is coincident with and essential to deconstructing the human. Although Wolfe above defined posthumanism as that which moves beyond the thematic treatment of posthuman sites, characters, events or factors in cultural artefacts, it is nevertheless true that the thematic presence of animals in literature, film, art, history or any other field often leads to, or contributes to, posthumanist readings, bolstering posthumanism's visibility and adding to its possible expressions. The same might be said for ecocriticism: its desire to establish the sources or causes of ecological crisis in the present by examining literature's representation of the environment, and human and non-human nature is ultimately about investigating the destructive consequences of anthropocentrism. Yet ecocriticism can lead to analysis that is utterly humanist in its conclusions: for example, the debate over how, or whether, to use the designation of 'the Anthropocene' (the term was first floated by chemist Paul Crutzen in 2000) to describe a geological era that is characterized by human transformation of the environment raises questions about how anti-anthropocentric ecological criticism is. Whether the Anthropocene counts as a true geological period is a matter for vigorous argument among scientists, but for many, especially for those in the environmental humanities, it usefully foregrounds the recent magnified impact human beings have had on the planet through mass extinctions, climate change, pollution and other factors. At the same time, however, it can be viewed as the ultimate anthropocentric concept, elevating human beings above all other life across millennia: only *we* have been able to accomplish this, of all the kinds of influences before us. Perhaps as important, the terminology hints that only we humans, among all our fellow creatures, are self-aware and possess language, and therefore are able to recognize our impact and name it after ourselves. This is, of course, the same kind of hubris that led to our ecological crisis in the first place. Both ecostudies and animal studies can demonstrate the stickiness of humanism when they fail to fully move away from either thematics or human exceptionalist frameworks. Both also provide evidence of why it is important to understand that posthumanism might even profitably embrace forms of humanism: where theoretical approaches motivated by activism are concerned, as are animal studies and ecocriticism, philosophical arguments have to be balanced against the ability to motivate in the often political and often unreconstructedly humanist world beyond the domain of theory. If that requires a little strategic exceptionalism, then a careful assessment of its value is better than wholesale erasure. Nevertheless, the humanist exceptionalism that makes us responsible for the damage we have done, whether to animal species particularly or to the whole planet, is not something we can simply expunge or mitigate, but must carefully deconstruct lest it creep back in through what we thought were locked doors.

Animal studies and ecocriticism relocate non-human beings, systems and phenomena at the centre of literary and cultural inquiry, correspondingly decentring the human as the proper focus for scholarship and criticism. This can go a long way toward accomplishing the relocation of the human Latour and other posthumanists advocate. Latour's Actor Network Theory (ANT), Object-Oriented Ontology (OOO), the new vitalism, object-oriented feminism, and other variations of what has come to be called the new materialisms likewise transform how we think about human beings by situating them as part of a web, a process of becoming, a network or an assemblage. ANT grew out of the intersections of sociology and science: as Latour describes it, the need for a new social theory began to emerge as science and technology either created or discovered the agency of what had once seemed merely things: 'non-humans – microbes, scallops, rocks and ships – presented themselves to social theory in a new way' as fellow actants, 'not simply the bearers of symbolic projection' (2005: 10). Heterogeneous entities mutually interact, shape the conditions for being and action, and at any moment are both acting and acted upon. This approach 'flattens' the social so that it does not refer only to human activity, but includes objects, non-human entities, processes and so on, all equally knit together to produce the network that is only reductively named 'the social'. Jane Bennett's vitalism, for instance, describes assemblages as

> ad hoc groupings of diverse elements, of vibrant materials of all sorts. Assemblages are living, throbbing confederations that are able to function despite the persistent presence of energies that confound them from within. They have uneven topographies ... and so power is not distributed equally across its surface. Assemblages are not governed by any central head: no one materiality or type of material has sufficient competence to determine consistently the trajectory or impact of the group. (2010: 23–4)

Bennett's vibrant entities enable things to happen without the governing consciousness that humanism would assume must be present.

The new materialisms represent a return to ontology after the philosophical and theoretical detours of epistemology. That is, new materialisms ask *what is an object* and rather than back up into the bottomless pit represented by the usual question *how do I know* what the object is/that the object exists, they assert the givenness of reality, and hence objects (even if these must remain in some way speculative). In this respect, new materialisms may resist the solipsism of much philosophical thought, and restore a world that is more diverse, more alive, and demands a more evolved acknowledgement. Levi Bryant points out that the binary of (knowing) subject/(known) object is at the root of the distortions of most philosophical inquiry: the answer is not to simply invert the binary, but to undo it, turning 'the subject into one object among many others, undermining its privileged, central, or foundational place within philosophy... As a consequence we get the beginnings of what antihumanism and post-humanism ought to be' (2011: 22–3). Nor can objects be reduced to their relations to human beings, or even to one another (that is to say that I don't only know that objects exist because one has hit me on the head, I know they exist as a general principle); and neither can the knowledge of objects be reduced to what Quentin Meillassoux calls correlationism – that is the premise that I only know the thing that hit me on the head because I can think in the first place, and when I think about that object or any other it is only real or true for me, and so is essentially not fully objectively there beyond me (2008). If Bryant found that the subject/object binary is at the root of philosophy's problems, Meillassoux asserts that this correlationist trap is also fundamental to and an obstruction in Western philosophy from Descartes forward.

Other 'speculative realists' like Meillassoux, including Graham Harman and Ian Bogost, explore the problem that objects (which include humans, things, processes, concepts, institutions and just about everything else one could list) nevertheless continue to pose metaphysics. Objects indeed can never be fully known by whatever consciousness interacts with them; yet they aren't diminished by that fact. An object's existence, its reality or presence, is not constrained by its relation to a human being, for instance, or even its ability to make something happen to or for another object (Harman 2002). Bogost embraces figurative language, especially analogical expression, to understand the perspective of things themselves – only through the often-despised process of imagining *likeness* can we create what he calls an 'alien phenomenology' (2012). Whatever the distinct lines of analysis or the varied answer to the 'question of the object', what unifies the new materialisms is a commitment to dethroning the human subject in favour of a horizontal and therefore flatter, if not completely undifferentiated, world.

Of course, the human entities of this materialist landscape have bodies, senses and cognition, all of which are coproduced by meshes or networks in which they are entangled. Unlike the Enlightenment body, which was imagined as bounded, enclosed, singular, able, a machine that does the will and is the 'container' of the 'mind', posthuman bodies are 'Queer, cyborg, metametazoan, hybrid, PWA; bodies-without-organs, bodies-in-process, virtual' and 'thrive in the mutual deformations of totem and taxonomy' (Halberstam and Livingston 1995: 19).[7] As Elizabeth Grosz puts it, 'the body is a most peculiar "thing," for it is never quite reducible to being merely a thing; nor does it ever quite manage to rise above the status of thing' (1994: xi). The body cannot be fully expressed through constructivist theories that posit it as the byproduct of language, discourse or culture; it is both what those theories say it is, and something – or some things – else. Phenomenological accounts of the body argue that its operations precede and determine the nature of epistemology. For instance, according to Maxine Sheets-Johnstone we only know anything in the first place through movement. Indeed, we have no selves before movement: 'We come straightaway moving into the world; we are precisely not *stillborn* ... *We literally discover ourselves in movement*. We grow kinetically into our bodies' (2011: 117). Brian Massumi begins with a similar insight: 'When I think of my body and ask what it does to earn that name, two things stand out. It *moves*. It *feels*' (2002: 1). Massumi distinguishes the body's physiological responsiveness from what we call 'emotion', which is 'the sociolinguistic fixing of the quality of an experience which is from that point onward defined as personal' (28); affects are instead sensory perspectives anchored in the body (35) but autonomous, the body's 'feelings' or responses to stimuli prior to being invested with meaning. Massumi discusses orientation in terms of architecture (177–207), while queer phenomenologist Sarah Ahmed (2006) analyses orientation in its bodily and sexual contexts, but both are concerned with the body's negotiations of internal and external environments.

For Stacy Alaimo, what matters is dismantling our assumption that there *is* an outside and an inside, a body and an environment that remain somehow separated or distinct from one another. Alaimo argues for the idea of transcorporeality, the ways in which environments move through bodies just as bodies do through environments: indeed, the two are continuous, not distinct. Alaimo is inspired by feminism, queer theory and disability studies, all of which challenge the legacy of the humanist body. Despite her focus on a human body, however, Alaimo insists that transcorporealism need not be anthropocentric if it undoes the disconnections of the humanist body and 'cultivate[s] a sense of tangible connection to the world to encourage an environmentalist ethos' (2010: 16). That is likewise true of the many strands of phenomenological thought cited above. Like the ontological work of the new materialisms, new phenomenologies reject the dead end of asking only how we know things or the world, and instead consider the body's engagement in its environment as a sensing, voyaging, responsive, embodied subject/object or quasi-thing.[8] That shift enables an attention to the non-human, to ecosystems and ecologies composed of many kinds of bodies, substances, phenomena or processes.

As do posthumanists, body-theorists trace several distinct lines of inheritance, some following a philosophical tradition descended from Edmund Husserl, Henri Bergson and Maurice Merleau-Ponty, others inspired by feminist or queer theory, still others by the neurosciences. These last argue for the embodied basis for all cognitive function. There is no such thing as a 'mind' that is separate from the body that contains or grounds its operations, no one-way street leading from minds to construct culture, literature, government and so on. Andy Clark argues that 'the squishy thing' inside the skull only becomes what is later branded a 'mind' because it is already a cyborg, even before it invents technologies to extend or enhance it (2004: 5). Reason, rather than existing prior to and separate from all other sensory inputs, as Descartes wanted to believe, is dependent on the body and its environment. Clark argues that 'human thought and reason is born out of looping interactions between material brains, material bodies, and complex cultural and technological environments. We create these supportive environments, but they create us too' (Clark 2004: 11). Embodied cognition (the way thought happens only through the body), distributed cognition (the argument that the 'mind' is composed of multiple platforms inside and outside the body), and situated cognition (the idea that thought occurs only through action) all shake up humanism's celebration of reason and the mind, displacing these operations away from the individual, and embedding them in a networked environment. The 'mind' is a fiction, a convenience for describing something much more diffuse, more complex, and less autonomous than humanism imagined it to be.

The conjunction of biological and sociological models in recent theory has allowed figures like Niklas Luhmann to describe the process of communication between individuals or groups and the environment. Like a cell, social entities have boundaries that divide one from another, and each from the relatively more chaotic environment outside itself. A system (social or cellular) maintains itself via *autopoiesis* (literally, self-making), the production of more communication via a sorting process to determine what the system considers meaningful. If autopoiesis stops, the system does too, and becomes once more merely environment. Human beings, however, are incidental, secondary to these social systems, which have ontological status in themselves – humans are thus paradoxically at once the social system's environment, and at the same time they exist *within* that environment. In Hans-Georg Moeller's explanation, humans are sidelined by the very thing we might think of as most 'human', our capacity for communication: 'human beings do not and cannot communicate – only communication can' (2006: 6). In contrast to a Cartesian philosophy that dictates the mind controls the body, mind and body in systems theory are both systems and cannot therefore control one another. 'The human being "as such" has no theoretical place in systems theory' since a human being is the fictional construct describing discrete and incommensurate things, like a social being, a biological being, a mental or intellectual being (Moeller 2006: 10). In other words, like the other theoretical paths we've travelled, systems theory accomplishes Latour's relocation of 'the human', in this case by rendering it part of, and in many ways subordinated to multiple types and levels of systems.

This very partial and incomplete overview of some of posthumanism's methods and schools of thought leaves out more than it includes, a sign of posthumanism's growth and diversity. Its goal, however, is to give a small glimpse of what undergirds the chapters to come. We turn next to the issue of Shakespeare's relevance to posthumanism, and vice versa, and to the truncated history that we have so far been working with.

What's he to Hecuba or Hecuba to him

In some of the guises I've outlined above, posthumanist theory has already taken up residence in Shakespeare studies. Animals, the environment, objects, cognition, body studies, affect theory: a significant amount of recent work on Shakespeare, other Renaissance writers, and early modern history and culture more broadly, has come out of interest in these topics. Thus, there are a huge number of monographs and collections on Shakespeare that 'count' as posthumanist, far too many to cite here. Few such works, however, have self-consciously branded themselves posthumanist, regardless of how compatible their approaches are with the theory or how deeply posthumanist theory informs their readings. Only a few recent collections announce posthumanist theory as a principal commitment: they include Stefan Herbrechter and Ivan Callus's *Posthumanist Shakespeares* (2012), Jean Feerick and Vin Nardizzi's *The Indistinct Human in Renaissance Literature* (2012) and Joseph Campana and Scott Maisano's *Renaissance Posthumanism* (2016).[9] In addition, some posthumanist theory offers readings of Shakespeare – Herbrechter's *Posthumanism: A Critical Analysis* (2013), for instance, returns repeatedly to the plays as examples, while a chapter in Bruce Clark's *Posthuman Metamorphosis* (2008) uses *A Midsummer Night's Dream* to illustrate systems theory. Still, the congeniality of the conjunction of Shakespeare and posthumanist theory may not be immediately evident to everyone: what does a sixteenth-century playwright have to do with twentieth- and twenty-first-century cybernetics, philosophy, systems or social theory? As Hamlet might ask, what's he to Hecuba, or Hecuba to him – what justifies dressing Shakespeare up in posthumanist attire and making him passionately speak for or about posthumanism?

Indeed, the 'post' in posthumanist theory seems to suggest that it can have little to do with what came before the present. Yet as a number of writers point out, that 'post' doesn't necessarily name a historical moment (although it can) as much as it suggests an outgrowth, or perhaps a kind of implosion of humanism's core concepts. 'It is inevitable that with "the invention of the human" the posthuman as one of his or her "others" also becomes thinkable, representable, possible, necessary' (Herbrechter 2013: 57). Feerick and Nardizzi describe the 'potential for human indistinction' as the 'dark underside of Renaissance celebration of man's preeminent place within the cosmos' (2012: 2). Posthumanism can therefore be thought of, as Campana and Maisano argue, as having 'its roots in and remain[ing] an offshoot of "Renaissance humanism"'

(2016: 2). For Herbrechter and Callus, posthumanism 'does not imply a simple turning away, either from humanism or from theory, but rather a continued "working through" or a "deconstruction" of humanism' (3).[10]

Here it's worth thinking a bit more about the difference between Enlightenment philosophy and Renaissance humanism. Unlike Enlightenment thought, which coalesced around a set of fairly consistent issues that constitute something we think of as 'modernity', Renaissance humanism was, as Campana and Maisano point out, 'never a coherent or singular worldview, much less a rallying cry for "man as the measure" – or the center – "of all things"' (2016: 2). They take to task figures like Braidotti and Wolfe for creating a 'Vitruvian straw man' (3), a misreading that substitutes a set of caricatures – 'posterboys for anthropological optimism' (Gouwens 2016: 39) – for the full range of early humanist ideas and positions. What humanism was for early moderns, they remind us, was an engagement with classical literatures of the past – close reading in effect, which is something they argue we should once again privilege. Rather than autonomy, disembodiment and transcendent authority, a close reading of Renaissance humanism turns up conflict over just these things when early humanists revisit over and over again certain salient texts.[11] Feerick and Nardizzi note that scholars of early modern literature have 'demonstrated the value of ecocritical paradigms for explicating the fraught nature of "the human"' (2012: 5) and other presentist concerns, and what may be more important, offer positive models of boundary-confusion and hierarchies that turn out to be profitably tangled (2012: 4). Prior to the disciplinary separation of science, political theory, religion and other ways of interpreting the world – before, that is, Boyle and Hobbes, the figures Latour focuses on – the connections among human and non-human things could be a source of marvel at the rich interdependencies of life, or wonder at God's great pattern for the cosmos. Renaissance humanism did not (always) seek to extract humanity from the mesh of beings in the world. Kenneth Gouwens suggests that recovering a more accurate picture of Renaissance humanism can be crucial in furthering the interests of posthumanist theory by making it 'more than just a genealogical antecedent', a fixed, reduced, closed set of texts and ideas against which we can rebel (2016: 54). Instead, reading more carefully in the works of past humanists might complicate our picture of the past, and open up lost avenues and paths for challenging Enlightenment humanism's hegemony.

Campana and Maisano's model for the obsessive reader is Milton, who concentrated as much on scripture as classical texts. Milton represents humanity's ideal state as lost at the moment of the expulsion from Eden; as they put it, '"our Grand Parents" … *flunked* obedience training' meaning that disembodiment and autonomy 'never were – and never will be – part of the human condition' (2016: 15). Can we say similar things about Shakespeare, who, while clearly the beneficiary of a good education and some thorough grounding in religion, was hardly as obsessed with Protestant theology as was Milton? Herbrechter and Callus summarize Shakespeare's positioning as literary and cultural theory's quintessential humanist: long before Harold Bloom's *Shakespeare and the Invention of the Human* (1999), or Robin Headlam Wells's *Shakespeare's Humanism* (2005) attempted to recirculate Shakespeare as the answer to assaults from feminism, historicism and cultural studies, Shakespeare served as the touchstone for humanist values. There are, however, as many Shakespeares as there are readers of Shakespeare. 'Shakespeare' has become something of an empty icon, appropriable by nearly anyone for anything (Herbrechter and Callus 2012); but one reason for that malleability is that in writing for the theatre Shakespeare worked in a multifaceted medium that served many agendas, and created an adaptable set of internally diverse texts. In other words, Shakespeare has always been dressed up in different costumes and tricked out in others' attire, has been used to shore up incompatibly varied ideological positions. 'Shakespeare' is, as is Hamlet's Hecuba, the product of multiple authors and agents – of actors, of layers of rhetoric, of gestures and allusions. But the result is, again as in Hamlet's case, to inspire his audience to new kinds of thought and action. Herbrechter and Callus describe 'retrofitting' Shakespeare, allowing new articulations of new and old (2012: 12–13) to mobilize the plays and poems yet again to new discourses and new ends. We have then, two answers to the question of what Hecuba is to him, what Shakespeare provides posthumanist theory: first that Shakespeare as a pre-Enlightenment figure might reflect a humanism not yet narrowed and rationalized, and therefore provide glimpses of possibilities shut down by the Enlightenment; and second that because of Shakespeare's status as cultural icon, and the works' heterogeneity, Shakespeare can be a useful tool for posthumanist theory.

But what's he to Hecuba? That is, what does posthumanist theory offer Shakespeare studies? That is a question less often asked, probably because the answers seem obvious: renewed relevance, a jolt of excitement for a profession engaged in analysing the corpus, the pleasures of discovery, the rewards of doing more recognizably ethical scholarship, inclusion in the presentist political agendas of ecostudies or animal studies. Getting theory to '[put] its ear to the ground and [listen] to the new sounds' of technology, cognitive science, environmental science, biology, zoology, geology and so on (Herbrechter and Callus 2012: 5) also means an expansion of the archive in which scholars of Shakespeare can work. New disciplinary crossings accompany new archaeologies of historical documents: Erica Fudge has, for instance, turned to wills and other legal documents detailing early moderns' relationships to their cattle to uncover the 'joint dance of being' among human and non-human creatures (2016: 146); Rebecca Totaro examines early modern meteorological treatises for how they inform the plays (forthcoming); Ben Bertram re-reads writers concerned with military matters from a completely new perspective and finds that they and Shakespeare agree that armies are assemblages that resist privileging the humans among them (forthcoming). Reflected through posthumanist theory, the landscape of Shakespeare studies changes, its contours shift and its woods and rivers and mountains coalesce, dissolve, migrate and reconstitute themselves. Such mutability, as any early modern could have told us, is a source of renewable energy, a sustainable resource, life itself, conceived not in opposition to death, but in cooperation with it.

Chapter designs

In the chapters that follow, I give a brief overview of both posthumanist theory's current inroads into Shakespeare scholarship, and at the same time construct readings that can serve as examples of how a posthumanist approach to issues in the plays and poems might work. In some chapters, that means a good deal of summary introduces the reader to the many kinds of scholarship that can be called posthumanist, followed by a very brief reading of a play – for chapters on animal studies, or bodies and minds, for instance, there is an abundance of material to synthesize, which leaves a bit less space for a how-to lesson. In a few cases, as with posthumanist cosmology, the examples of existing scholarship are fewer and so are more easily subordinated to a reading of a text. It's not my intent to give a comprehensive account of all the ways posthumanist theory 'happens' in the scholarship, but rather to touch on what I consider important highlights, indicate through my summaries where further reading would be rewarding, and then offer something original to readers that puts the theory into practice.

It is tempting to end with some laudatory comments that suggest that the conjunction of Shakespeare and posthumanist theory will offer better or more effective redress against the destructive aspects of modernity, or will cure or ameliorate its self-deceptions and 'irreparable crimes' (Latour 1993: 125). Posthumanist theory should itself qualify and dampen such utopian idealism and highlight the exceptionalism that it rests on. And yet, even the most confirmed posthumanist theorist is motivated by the impulse to transform and improve human beings – if not the beings themselves, then their effects on their fellow creatures and on the places we have to live. What posthumanism actually does, according to Wolfe, is to describe more minutely and accurately the human, to account for 'its characteristic modes of communication, interaction, meaning, social signification, and affective investments with *greater* specificity', but with the result that we attend more to our 'finitude and dependency' (2010: xxv, xxvi). We do not escape ourselves by becoming posthuman or posthumanist. And so this volume seeks only to draw the outlines of a map, and not to force the map to tell us where the treasure is or even if there's a treasure to be had at all. It has designs on the reader, but it does not offer a grand design, lest it reproduce the very thing it remains sceptical towards.

2

Posthuman Cosmography

'It is the stars above us / govern our conditions', says Kent in *King Lear* (4.3.33–4) in a scene that follows a series of catastrophes: Lear's banishment of Cordelia, his subsequent descent into madness after his remaining daughters' extreme cruelty, and his raving amidst violent storms on the heath, not to mention Gloucester's blinding, and Edmund's treasonous plotting. Kent struggles lamely to explain how such diverse 'issue' as Cordelia, Goneril and Regan could arise from 'self mate and mate' (4.3.35–6), but his faith in some supernatural force that maintains order in nature and humanity strikes an audience as feeble, impotent in the face of the play's events. In this, he joins his contemporary, Gloucester, who also believes that cosmological oddities have meaning for human events ('These late eclipses in the sun and moon portend no good to us' he says in 1.2.103–4): both men are relics of Lear's generation, incapable of responding effectively to the new world in which they live. In contrast, Edmund rejects supernatural explanations, remarking on his father's superstition 'This is the excellent foppery of the world, that when we are sick in fortune, often the surfeits of our own behavior, we make guilty of our disasters the sun, the moon, and stars' (1.2.118–121). But if *King Lear* seems to pit superstitious elders against their violently rational offspring, the play refuses to simply endorse rational science over and against belief in magic or miracle: Edgar's timely – one might say, miraculous – transformation out of his disguise as Poor Tom, and into a noble challenger come to destroy his bastard half-brother lets him levy the charge that Edmund has committed treason against the gods. Indeed, Edgar's victory is coloured with the language of divine retribution: 'The gods are just, and of our pleasant vices / Make instruments to plague us' (5.3.168–9). Edmund bows to this interpretation: 'The wheel is come full circle' (5.3.172) he responds, crediting the same fortune and fate – what Kent terms 'the judgment of the heavens' (5.3.235) – that he denied and against which he had raged all along.

Elsewhere, Shakespeare likewise uses the stars in various, and sometimes contradictory ways. To explain what seems a tragedy of mainly human manufacture in *Romeo and Juliet*, the Chorus tells us the young lovers are 'star-crossed', doomed not by the intransigence of the feuding kinship networks that drive that play's plot, but by the accident of plague and a delayed message (Pro. 6). In *1 Henry IV*, Owen Glendower believes that the cosmic omens attending his birth mean he is destined for greatness, although Hotspur mocks him for his superstition; in *Richard II*, a captain emphatically names meteors along with other natural and human phenomena as proof that the king is dead (2.4.8–10), only to turn out to be quite wrong. In *Twelfth Night*, Sir Toby attributes Sir Andrew's shapely leg to its formation under the star of a 'galliard' (1.2.115) mistaking the links between the sign of Taurus and 'legs and thighs' (see Tillyard 1961: 7–8). An eclipse signifies Antony's fate in *Antony and Cleopatra* (3.13.158–9) and throughout the plays planets become unmoored, wandering and causing plagues (*Troilus and Cressida* 1.3.94–101; *Winter's Tale* 2.1.105–7; *Timon of Athens* 4.3.1–3). What Laurie Shannon has described as a 'queer cosmography' in *Lear* seems to apply more broadly to a range of plays, albeit with divergent degrees of credibility (2011: 171–8). So what do we conclude: that Shakespeare believed in the influence of the planets and stars, or not? That he referenced such belief as a touchstone for simple-minded gullibility, or that he deployed the language of astrology and the motions of the heavens as code for the theological truths he was prevented by the censors from offering on stage? Is there a consistent relationship between characters and the non-human forces that seem to drive their actions, and if so what might it say about the status of the 'human' in the plays?

This chapter takes up a few of the many ways Shakespeare's cosmos relies on, questions, adapts and propagates systems, theories and relations between forces larger than, or sometimes entirely alien to, human beings, and it models how a posthumanist reading foregrounds these to arrive at a new set of insights into the play. Posthumanist theory puts 'the human' as a functional category into sceptical abeyance in part through an examination of the vital interconnections with non-human forces and beings that make and unmake individuals and humanity as a whole. For early moderns, these interconnections included the sway that celestial objects held over earth and its inhabitants. Far from exhibiting an imperial 'I', self-governing and self-authorizing, Shakespeare's characters often seem battered and perplexed by their embeddedness in a world of unstable, random effects – earthquakes, meteors, eclipses, wandering planets, motions of the moon, the tides, storms, cold and heat. In other words, Shakespeare's characters often strongly resemble posthumanist theorists' articulations of human subjects that emerge from chaos, rather than mastery, and are endlessly in process, rather than fixed and static. In Shakespeare's most nihilistic play, *King Lear*, social and religious structures that promise to extract human beings from their messy entanglements with nature or with embodied being fail miserably. That failure is linked to a cosmology which does not cooperate in producing human sovereignty as the byproduct of some distant but powerful force – whether God, or the stars, or nature, or any other similar guarantor of category coherence.

We now think of astrology and astronomy as occupying completely different dimensions of thought, the one mere superstition, the other clearly science. Belief in astrological control over human and natural events might therefore seem incompatible with the apparent rational bias of early modern humanism, but the two dwelt comfortably together for some time. Early modern providentialism, the idea that all things evidenced God's guiding hand in the workings of the world, ensured that the mechanical motions of the stars and planets, and their influence on human affairs, could be reconciled with one another relatively easily. Astronomy and astrology were closely related also because both concerned the heavens and the cosmos, and so prominent scientists like Copernicus and Kepler, and philosophers like Ficino, engaged in astrological projects. While the Catholic Church prosecuted practitioners for the use of magic, empiricists like Bacon saw astrology as simply another domain of rational science, one expression of the laws of 'nature' that would ultimately come under human control: the members of Salomon's House in *The New Atlantis* stipulate that 'The end of our Foundation is the knowledge of Causes, and secret motions of things; and the enlarging of the bounds of Human Empire, to the effecting of all things possible' (1996: 480). Where there was resistance among the new philosophers, it came largely from the sense that belief in supernatural or magical forces diminished human potential: Pico della Mirandola, for instance, wrote strenuously against the discipline in his *Disputations Against Astrology*, condemning its denial of free will, which he saw as the cornerstone of the humanist agenda.

The model of a universe that reveals itself to human understanding through empirical observation, offering its secrets to enhance the exercise of human agency and ensure human salvation, appears in much criticism of Renaissance culture and literature. First published in the 1940s, E. M. W. Tillyard's account of the Elizabethan World Picture, which built extensively on A. O. Lovejoy's 1936 *The Great Chain of Being*, made the case for continuity with medieval versions of cosmic order, 'an ordered universe arranged in a fixed system of hierarchies but modified by man's sin and the hope of his redemption' (1961: 5–6). Tillyard described a set of correspondences between planes of creation: 'the divine and angelic, the universe or macrocosm, the commonwealth or body politic, man or the microcosm, and the lower creation'.

Mankind, however, held a special position, he was 'the nodal point ... [that] had the unique function of binding together all creation, of bridging the greatest cosmic chasm, that between matter and spirit' (1961: 83, 66).

Tillyard's thesis has been so widely criticized for its inaccuracy, its distortions and omissions, its problematic ideological utility, that it is not worth tracing its fate here; suffice to say that it fell out of favour for decades. Yet the model of an orderly, integrated cosmos that it describes, one that emphasizes connections and correspondences as much as rigid hierarchies, has been recuperated by some scholars with ecologically informed agendas. Gabriel Egan, for instance, has advocated re-appropriating and renewing a Tillyardian system of correspondences between macro- and microcosms for its insistence on a 'unitary Earth, or Gaia', a single self-regulating organism that functions comparably to the body of an individual human (2006: 29). James Lovelock's Gaia hypothesis has a mixed history among scientists and environmentalists, but to Egan its emphasis on the interconnection and interdependence of organic and non-organic life is worth mobilizing in the interests of current debates about ecological destruction. While he is clear that Gaia theory is not directly descended from an Elizabeth 'picture' of creation, Egan suggests that it shares enough resonances with (Tillyard's version of) Shakespeare's cosmological views that it might be worth returning to the plays to consider what alternatives to Enlightenment rational science we might find in them. Todd Borlik is willing to trace the classical and early modern prehistory of the Gaia hypothesis, even though he admits it is impossible to empirically verify (2011: 28). Pythagoras, he finds, was the first person 'to lend intellectual respectability to the idea that the earth is a living creature', and through his philosophy, 'early moderns were capable of imagining a unity that was not macrotranscendant', that is, that did not set reason and science in mastery over nature; rather, early moderns had intellectual traditions that allowed a sense of 'reciprocity' and therefore gratitude and stewardship toward non-human beings (2011: 34, 74).

One criticism of the Gaia model notes its tendency to erase or downplay disequilibrium and randomness. Likewise, a Tillyardian pleasure in harmony and stability can lead to overestimations of early modern confidence in immutable natural law. Tillyard himself noted that the drama, mainly Shakespeare's, might seem to refute the picture he was drawing, but insisted that it was 'so taken for granted, so much part of the collective mind of the people, that it is hardly mentioned except in explicitly didactic passages' (1961: 9). A number of posthumanist ecocritics resist the appeal of balance, harmony and comprehensibility that attends the idea of 'equilibrium' or nature's organic wholeness, to posit instead a Shakespearean cosmos that takes as its norm the chaotic and unhinged mutations of the elements and of beings (gods, goddesses, fairies) that early moderns so feared. In other words, these critics suggest that the Elizabethan World Picture involved a good bit of whistling into the void. When Steve Mentz, for instance, reads the same speech by Ulysses in *Troilus and Cressida* that Tillyard uses as a lynchpin of his argument, he finds it is not, as Tillyard saw it, an expression of the interconnected relations that guarantee an inalterable cosmic harmony, but a register of how disordered the world tends to be:

> ... The heavens themselves, and this centre
> Observe degree, priority, and place,
> Insisture, course, proportion, season, form,
> Office, and custom, in all line of order.
> And therefore is the glorious planet Sol
> In noble eminence inthroned and sphered
> Amidst the other, whose med'cinable eye
> Corrects the ill aspects of planets evil
> And posts, like the commandment of a king,
> Sans check, to good and bad. But when the planets
> In evil mixture to disorder wander,
> What plagues and what portents, what mutiny,
> What raging of the sea, shaking of earth,
> Commotion in the winds, frights, changes, horrors,

Divert and crack, rend and deracinate
The unity and married calm of states
Quite from their fixture!
(1.3.85–101)

To Tillyard, Ulysses' speech weds 'cosmic and domestic', lining up the sun with kings and fathers: 'the bounded waters / Should lift their bosoms higher than the shores' and 'the rude son should strike his father dead' (1.3.111–12, 115) if this order is contravened (Tillyard 1961: 10). But Mentz sees here an account of 'disorder and lack of harmony' that, rather than 'represent[ing] deviations from natural order, instead pinpoint the speech's beyond-natural portrayal of the nonhuman environment' (2016: 335). Inviting us to take to heart the speech's use of images of storms at sea, Mentz argues that 'Supplementing natural harmony with oceanic dynamism transforms a speech about stable hierarchy into a complex vision of multiply entangled systems' (335). Such a reading exemplifies the 'swimmer poetics' Mentz advocates elsewhere as a suitable posture for facing current ecological crisis – in the Anthropocene, where we experience the destruction and dislocation of global warming, we must become accustomed to riding out storms, and navigating the ever-changing ocean currents (Mentz 2012). Shakespeare, for Mentz, is 'the poet for whom all natural things become pliable, artificial, and changeable', and therefore the plays' irreducible variety of positions on issues like the nature of the cosmos or the cosmic order of nature results in a 'dynamic and unsustainable vision of nature that appears neither very green nor exclusively human' (2016: 334). Thinking about our current ecological condition, Mentz mobilizes the image of shipwreck, so dear to Shakespeare's heart in plays ranging from *Twelfth Night* to *The Tempest*, and lurking in Ulysses' speech in his choice of the image of a 'raging sea', 'commotion in the winds', that 'divert' or change a vessel's course. Shipwreck describes a posthuman condition that we moderns are beginning to experience anew: we are wet, touched everywhere by the inhuman elements of wind and water; we are shaken by catastrophe, disoriented and excluded from dry land. That catastrophe is not one about to happen but one that is already happening as 'the vessels that have carried us this far are coming to pieces under our feet' (2015: 163). But there is always the possibility of survival and recovery, riding the waves like a swimmer, in order to dry out via retrospective narratives.

Had he taken parts of Lovejoy's extended analysis in *The Great Chain of Being* more to heart, Tillyard might have recognized that it already provided a counterargument to any version of a harmonious and organic world order in the plays. Chaos, disorder, and mutability were sources of fear that this entire system, 'the law of nature', might 'cease functioning' (Lovejoy 1964: 16). Lovejoy emphasizes moments when Shakespeare and others echo medieval theology's sense of the world as a burden, an encumbrance that weighs down the aspirant soul. The earth, next only to Hell as the centre of the universe, was the locus of 'filth and mire', and thus did not deserve to associate with the purer sun, moon and starts that moved so beautifully above (102).[1] The advent of modernity has always assumed a degree of success in suppressing or banishing the sheer material drag of being a created thing; thus Descartes's formulation of the cogito, exemplary of (some would say foundational to) Enlightenment scepticism, requires the absolute dissociation of the mind from matter and the body. But, as we saw in Chapter 1, Bruno Latour has argued that this version of modernity was never actually fully realized, leaving us endlessly struggling to 'purify' objects and situate them on one side or the other of the nature/culture divide, making them either subjects or objects, consciousness or matter (1993). Instead, Latour observes, hybridity sneaks in the back door, over and over again. Latour's articulation of a modern project in which an unwritten, unacknowledged 'modern constitution' guarantees that the matter of science – nature, things outside the human or the social – never comingles with the domain of the human (politics, ideology, society) describes a system of thought that refuses to recognize the interpenetration, indeed the mutual construction, of 'nature' and 'culture', one that defines early modern Western philosophy since Descartes. Tillyard's schema of divinely ensured orderliness, although it wants to allow for the union of matter and spirit in mankind, does so at the expense of imposing a purifying impulse everywhere else. It therefore ends up expressing the desires and assumptions of its own time, rather than those of early modernity. Against modernity's imposition of order, posthumanist theory encourages the recapture of premodern oceanic tumult that we see in Mentz's work.

Lovejoy lists a set of 'truly revolutionary theses in cosmography' (1964: 108) in Shakespeare's world, none of which come from Copernicus or Kepler, and none of which were empirically verifiable, but which extended from medieval philosophical and religious ideas of plenitude. These include the belief that other planets were inhabited (decentring the earth as the locus of all God's creation); the dispersal of stars through a vaster firmament than had ever been imagined, and the ideas that stars were other suns like our own, both of which hinted at a universe with no shape or centre – that is, governed by no system at all.[2] Rather than shaken by astronomy and its advances, then, early moderns may well have been most disturbed by the very logic of the supposedly orderly world they inherited. The paradox in Lovejoy's analysis defeats the smug security of a Tillyardian order, and works strongly against the assumptions about scale that underwrite the Gaian model of the earth as a self-regulating organism (why this earth? Why it and not the universe as a whole? Self-regulating to what end and including what natural forces?). Posthumanist critics like Mentz embrace early modern writers like Shakespeare in the interests of uncovering not the glorious, harmonious equilibrium that anticipates Gaia theory, despite that theory's capacity to diminish human self-aggrandizement, but to mobilize overlooked or repressed narratives, stories that can 'dash early modern European triumphalism onto the rocks and tell a new story of cultural transformation' (2015: 10).

We might return now to Shakespeare's cosmos, to think differently about the way heavenly bodies are implicated in both individual behaviour and upheavals in nature. Shakespeare's characters are convinced that they are subject to events that are the byproduct of forces beyond human comprehension – the planets, the moon, the movement of the stars – and at the same time, living in a world in which those same forces might randomly disrupt what early moderns conceive as 'natural law'. What Tillyard called 'correspondences' are too often between completely incommensurate things, things that follow distinct and disordered trajectories. Raging seas and earthquakes are simply not the same as fathers struck dead by sons or states wracked by war. I read these moments in the plays for their suggestion that early modern theories of order attempted to explain, however imperfectly, the disorienting experiences associated with what Timothy Morton has called 'hyperobjects', 'things that are massively distributed in time and space relative to humans' (2013: 1; see also 2011: 209). Hyperobjects are non-local because they involve problems of scale, usually massively larger than humans can apprehend. They are viscous, meaning that they stick to beings that are 'involved' with them, infiltrating the flesh, blood and cells, and manifesting effects long after they might seem to be behind us. Hyperobjects exert themselves interobjectively: the mesh that includes hyperobjects also includes humans, or subjects which are really just a kind of object, as well as all the gaps and spaces between things. They produce weakness, the knowledge that there is no possibility any longer of a Nietzchean superman, but only of small, vulnerable mammals like humans that are 'tuned' to the entities that can destroy them (Morton 2013: 176). Morton asserts that they produce hypocrisy, in the sense of hidden messages about our doom that both reveal secrets about the hyperobject's existence, and lie to us about it (we see signs of them and the doom they bring, but never the thing itself); things like rain and sunburns and plastic bags all bear messages of the catastrophe of global warming, but they do not provide a place from which to decide on action. They lie and conceal even as they deliver their message. Finally, hyperobjects generate lameness because they do not coincide with themselves – no part of them is coincident with the whole – which extends to human beings who are 'hobbled from within' by being 'hermetically sealed from other entities' (2013: 196). The 'fragile inconsistency' (196) of lameness is necessary to existence, but also a loss of the illusion of wholeness.

While Morton is concerned with hyperobjects in the Anthropocene, he acknowledges that there have always been hyperobjects. Without tying my reading too much to the relative validity of Morton's specific choices and claims about hyperobjects in our present moment, I want to offer a posthumanist reading of *King Lear* that arises from the proposition that it is 'about' a set of hyperobjects – land, weather, and the conflict between or within the two as it is expressed through one of the period's more disruptive experiences, the earthquake. Through its allusions to earthquakes, the play gives us a set of characters suffering, and recognizing, their relation to hyperobjects – not cosmic order via constellations and their influence on the world, but terrifying events through which every system by which humans attempt to make meaning around them is rendered hollow.

I link these hyperobjects (land, weather and earthquake) because the play does so explicitly in terms of the failure of conceptual structures that are designed to explain or contain natural phenomena. Gloucester's reference to 'these late eclipses', and Edmund's sarcasm in response, channels his and the audience's discomfort with Lear's division of his land between his daughters; Kent's musings on Cordelia's impossible difference from her sisters (and hence their genetic relation and the certainties or uncertainties of sexual reproduction) likewise are conveyed via astrological theory. The terrific storm that accompanies Lear's banishment from the comforts of the social world seems to arise in tandem with his internal distress, confirming, as any number of critics have noted, the assumption among early moderns that as God's anointed, the monarch and the elements existed in a reciprocal relationship. It was exactly this assumption that coloured Elizabeth I's assertion that the storms that destroyed the Spanish Armada in 1588 were divinely directed: as the medal celebrating her victory announced, *Flavit Jehovah et Dissipati Sunt* (Jehovah blew with his winds, and they were scattered). Yet what seems a simple correspondence between planes of creation, à la Tillyard, turns out to veer away from such a clear principle, and the storm becomes something much harder to read, less Lear's doing, more the indifferent raging of something entirely hostile to humans, and uninterpretable by them. But I also argue that the play is, through all these moments, constantly addressing the very real bodily and psychic trauma of earthquake as a 'natural' calamity, alluding to historical events of the late sixteenth century at the same time that it links these to the catastrophe earthquake wreaks on ideological certainties of all sorts.

Weak, lame, hypocrite Lear

King Lear is a play about land. Its events are precipitated by Lear's attempt to divide his kingdom among his three daughters. Before anything can happen, Lear calls for a map (1.1.37) on which he will later indicate Goneril's portion: 'Of all these grounds, even from this line to this ... we make thee lady' (1.163–5). Henry S. Turner points out that this map is 'a "modern" idea of space as a quantifiable and measurable geometric abstraction' that becomes more and more abstract as the scene advances (1997: 172; see also Bozio 2015). While Goneril's land has 'shadowy forests and with champains riched / With plenteous rivers and wide-skirted meads', Regan's is 'this ample third of our fair kingdom, / No less in space, validity, and pleasure / Than that conferred on Goneril' (1.1.64–5; 80–2). Turner's analysis traces the play's representation of space from stage to page, both of which enact the undecidability of Lear's position, 'without' both the trappings that made him king, and without 'a fictional place that is itself barely visible and defined only negatively by attributes' (1997: 183). Turner adds a new dimension to the many resonances of Cordelia's term 'nothing', which comes to reflect the very conditions of stage and page; he also gives us a new framework for Lear's venture onto the 'heath' (which doesn't exist in the original play versions) and his experience of the storm, which puts him within the world his maps charted, but without the dominion over it he assumed in the first scenes. But I want to dwell a moment on the text that inspires Turner, namely A. C. Bradley's 1904 commentary on the play, in which Bradley registers the 'very vagueness in the sense of locality' and the 'sense of vastness, the feeling not of a scene or particular place, but of a world' that he thinks characterizes *Lear* (1904: 247). Bradley responds to the play's impossible geography not by trying to find local references to pin it down, but by understanding that the play deliberately constructs a placeless environment that takes the familiar and makes it feel alien. Morton, on the other hand, deploys hyperobjects to dispel the idea of a 'world' altogether, in favour of the return of 'the earth', since it is the concept of a world that has prevented our full engagement with ontology, rather than epistemology where objects are concerned. To have a *world* is to engage in the creation of a body of knowledge; while to encounter a hyperobject prevents the detours epistemology encourages, where denial and affective distance are possible, where human subjectivity is king and the earth merely an object to know (Morton 2013: 5–18). Though Bradley settles on the term 'world' in his search for language adequate to the experience of reading or watching *Lear*, Turner insists we should instead focus on the distance enforced by Lear's maps, his confidence in his possessive authority over the lands they indicate, which collapses just as completely as does Lear's social and political power upon his surrender of the throne. Wandering the material contours of the land he did not know – which, despite the best efforts of cartographical technology, he *could* not know – and battered by the 'fretful elements' (3.1.4) Lear moves just as 'feelingly' as the blind Gloucester, not through a landscape, which might offer a sense of the locality Bradley finds missing in the play, but through one face of the hyperobject that is the earth itself. Lear, in other words, encounters an object, discovers his entanglement with its phenomena, but cannot contain the experience through traditional rational modes of discourse. What Lear discovers is what it is like to undergo a 'being-quake', a fundamental recalibration of his sensory and intellectual existence.[3] The land, the earth, the elements that both chafe and feed it, exist without reference to Lear, without consideration of the human at all. The play establishes something like an early modern version of the sublime: not a Burkean submission to authority or the Kantian 'temporary cognitive failure' that leads to inner freedom, but an intimacy with the Other that does little more than humble and efface the human at the same time that it reveals the Other's ultimate unknowability (Morton 2011: 209).

Gloucester invokes eclipses to explain the King's 'fall ... from the bias of nature' and the 'mutinies', 'discord', 'treason' and the 'cracked' bond between fathers and sons (1.2.107–17). He dismisses science, 'the wisdom of nature that can reason it thus and thus' (1.2.105) and takes some perverse comfort in the inscrutability of Nature, which can't be fully explained by human knowledge. Yet it is exactly Gloucester's confidence that there *is* a thing humans can call Nature, an entity that exists and determines events, that the play assaults. Nor is Edmund, who contemptuously dismisses his father's faith, any better; he too calls on 'Nature', understood as the law of radical self-interest set in opposition to the dictates of culture and convention (1.2.1–4). The disappearance of Nature in favour of mere phenomena puts this play in tension with others that celebrate the Tillyardian correspondence between monarch and, for instance, weather. Duncan's death in *Macbeth*, which results in 'unruly' shaking of the earth (2.2.54, 61) or Leontes' realm made wintry through its ruler's self-defeating jealousy, repeat the climatological principle of correspondence that explained the defeat of the Spanish Armada. Certainly Lear thinks he and the weather have something to do with each other: 'Blow winds, and crack your cheeks! Rage, blow! / You cataracts and hurricanoes, spout / Till you have drenched our steeples, drowned the cocks!' (3.2.1–3). But Lear acts on nothing any more – he is weak, lame, revealed as a hypocrite (in the original sense of the term meaning acting *only* on the stage of social and political power) and exposed to the hypocrisy (in Morton's sense) of natural events that signal doom but always also put him in the wrong. He is neither the source nor the explanation for the storm; it is just a storm. It continues whether or not he is mad, and abuses those who are neither rulers nor victims of family treasons. He later realizes 'the thunder would not peace at my bidding' (4.6.101–2). Like the play's undecidable location, the storm belongs to no season, no particular climatological process; it simply *is*, a kind of 'everystorm' assaulting Lear's unaccommodated everyman. In fact, what the storm manifests most is the viscosity of weather, the capacity of phenomena to 'invade' the human *body* 'to the skin' (3.4.7), not some emergence from the 'spirit' of kingship or even the simple cycles identifiable in other plays' weather patterns.

This is not merely to say that something we could call 'nature' operates without reference to 'humankind'. It is to establish the earth and its weather as an object that refuses to be comprehended, to be either quantified or mythologized – yet one that is omnipresent, persistent, and invasive of bodies, human or otherwise. In Shannon's words, the rain in *Lear* is queer. It confuses, violates distinctions, rejects binarisms. Or, to borrow Sarah Ahmed's language about queer orientation instead, the play stages Lear's experience of 'throw[ing] the world up, or throwing the body from its ground' (2006: 157).

Lear's trajectory in the play has vexed critics: is he enlightened somehow by his experiences? Is there a transformation in his perspective on the world? These kinds of questions assume a universe dominated by issues of individual consciousness on the one hand, and epistemology on the other – or perhaps these are the same thing, since whether Lear 'grows' by the end of the play is dependent on his construction of some new epistemological system by which to interpret the phenomena of his world. But if we read the play in a posthumanist vein, according to my suggestion here, as the dismantling of the world itself, of systems by which worlds are made, then such questions make no sense. A reader concerned with how the play uses animals to establish the category 'human' would note, for instance, that whatever Lear seems to recognize about the instability or fictive nature of the category is undone when he carries Cordelia's body into the final scene, asking 'Why should a dog, a horse, a rat have life, / And thou no breath at all?' (5.3.312–3).[4] Human exceptionalism (or perhaps Cordelian exceptionalism) is reinstated, against the moments of insight that peppered Lear's suffering (Sheen 2004: 99–100). To return for a moment to Morton's schema, we might think about Lear's reaction to dead Cordelia as part of the encounter with a hyperobject: 'Hyperobjects are genuinely apocalyptic … in the sense that they *lift the veil* of prejudice – but in so doing they do not catapult us into a beyond. Rather they fix us more firmly to the spot, which is no longer an embeddedness in a world' (2013: 144) In the face of the hyperobject, no human recovery of all the things implied by a 'world' – the ability to overlay meaning on phenomena, to put the human at the centre of the cosmos, ideas like 'nature' and 'family' – is possible at all. Thus Lear remains stuck in the place, the soil, the clime the play never clearly names, lamenting the end of life, or possibly denying life itself, or maybe chiding it or asking it a question ('no, no, no life?' 5.3.311). Shut off from other entities, he posits a vision of Cordelia still breathing that no one else can see as he dies, leaving Kent to assert that 'he but usurped his life' (5.3.323).

Earthquake, being-quake

'Why in the world', asks A. C. Bradley in discussing *King Lear*, 'should Gloster [*sic*], when expelled from his castle, wander painfully all the way to Dover simply in order to destroy himself?' (1904: 257).[5] Bradley details the various geographical oddities and obscurities that characterize *Lear* in distinction to other tragedies, asking why, for instance,

Gloucester's castle seems to be located on some empty heath, and finally why after the several moves from castle to castle, 'afterwards they all drift towards Dover for the purpose of the catastrophe'. Indeed, Bradley is on to something: Dover is repeatedly, insistently invoked, particularly in Acts 3 and 4 as Gloucester stumbles blindly toward his hoped-for death, even though there seems little context for such specificity. In my view, Bradley answers his own question: Dover, for Shakespeare and his contemporaries, is historically associated with catastrophe. In particular, Dover might well have evoked audience memories of England's most recently experienced earthquake, the 1580 temblor that hit the Dover Straits.[6] Although contemporary reports focused mainly on the experiences of London and other major towns and cities, a large portion of Dover's cliffs sheared off (taking with it part of Dover castle), and local damage was extensive (Haslett and Bryant 2008). Folkestone, the town closest to the quake's epicentre, was just ten miles south of Dover's port, and thus the quake affected an important location for trade and military defence. Whether inspired somehow by the earthquake itself, or simply by the appalling condition of the port (because of severe storms and lack of funding or manpower, the mouth of the harbour had become so choked as to be nearly useless by the 1570s; see Statham 1899: 102), Walter Raleigh supposedly proposed its reconstruction in 1580, but works projects struggled with the engineering challenges of the strait and the harbour. In the *Discourse of Sea Ports*, we are offered a letter purporting to be from Raleigh to Elizabeth, in which he encourages the crown to compete with its rivals, Holland and Flanders, to construct 'Havens artificial' to facilitate trade and military dominance. But Henry Sheeres, editor of the 1700 publication of the *Discourse* recalls that in 1682 he spoke at length to King Charles II about repairing the port, which was yet once more fallen into decay, indicating that although 'the port of Dover has been the scene of some of the most varied and colossal engineering projects in history', none had yet triumphed over the forces of wind and water.[7]

Dover, in short, was a location associated both with the aspirations of English technology, but also with the catastrophic effects of earthquakes and storms, and thus with assaults on the premise that human industry could tame nature and make it serve human ends. Yet human endeavour did not cease after endless rounds of battle with earth and sea, nor did failure dampen the desires attached to its success – it was constantly narrativized (possibly at some point by Raleigh, with certainty by Thomas Digges and by Sheeres, but also by many others) as a site where engineering would somehow vanquish the elements. Indeed, Dover might stand as an emblem of the human relationship to the chaotic operations of the natural world – in other words, of human resilience in the face of repeated disaster. While not a scene exactly of shipwreck, Dover stands in the same place as the shipwreck narrators Mentz discusses, bringing a rhythm of devastation followed by salvage and repair to both the port's material form and to its potential to affirm human dominance over nature. All this, I argue, resonates through *Lear*'s location, through the play's action, and through the significance of both.

On 6 April 1580, at six in the evening, the quake hit England. It was much discussed in a series of pamphlets and shows up in poems, diaries and other sources; while the quake itself might not have been huge by modern standards (according to current estimates, it rang in at between five and six on the Richter scale, a level at which countries with modernized infrastructure experience less destruction), it was one of the largest to hit England – and what may well be more important, it conjured memories of other, relatively recent and massively destructive earthquakes in Lisbon and Constantinople, adding to the fear it inspired.[8] It was seized on by diverse groups of writers: Thomas Churchyard (1580) reported on the quake's consequences for humans and human-made infrastructure in London and nearby cities, while Gabriel Harvey used it as a satirical avenue into questions of logic and science.[9] The majority of writers, including James Yates (1582), Abraham Fleming, Arthur Golding and Richard Tarleton, viewed the quake as a warning from God, even a relatively gentle one (Churchyard writes 'this earthquake is but half a check', 1580: Sig. C1v). Tarleton's poem puts it this way, referencing other past disasters like seas that changed their tides, or great blizzards:

> But if these tokens which be past and gone
> Have took no root at all within your hearts,
> You needs must grant this earthquake to be one,
> Unless you challenge heaven for deserts,
> Our health of souls must hang in great suspense
> When earth and sea do quake for our offense.[10]

The uniform conclusion of the pamphleteers and poets was that God was chiding England for its pride and presumption, most clearly signalled in the fact that the earthquake did most of its damage to houses and churches: Churchyard points out 'those that stood in the highest rooms and standings' were most shaken by the tremor; and Tarleton warns 'set not thy glory upon sumptuous and stately buildings, which are subject to the wind' (Churchyard 1580: B2r; Campbell 1941: 297).

London and its environs produced quick literary reaction, but the direct effects of the quake were most powerful at sea and around the vicinity of Dover. Its epicentre is estimated to have been under the waters of the straits, approximately midway between England and the continent. Ships were destroyed, seas rose and tsunamis were spawned. At Calais, an observer recorded this description of the quake's impact:

> [T]he sea overflowed into the city and did ruin and drown a great number of houses, and numerous persons perished, and a great multitude of beasts lost which were at pasture outside this city. Mention hath been made of several ships that perished by the great and awful tempestuousness of the sea ... One passenger that came from Dover to Calais relates that his ship did touch the bottom of the sea five time, and the waves mounting higher than six heights of a spear above

his ship ... Several who crossed from England, leaving from the port of Dover, made mention that they thought themselves lost, and that there were similar shakings that way beyond the sea.[11]

Earthquakes, according to Aristotle and most early modern sources, were caused by the 'exhalations of the earth', or strong winds, in combination with rain. In his *Meteorology*, Aristotle writes:

> Now it is clear, as we have already said, that there must be exhalation both from moist and dry, and earthquakes are a necessary result of the existence of these exhalations. For the earth is in itself dry but contains much moisture because of the rain that falls on it; with the result that when it is heated by the sun and its own internal fires, a considerable amount of wind is generated both outside it and inside, and this sometimes all flows out, sometimes all flows in, while sometimes it is split up ... the substance most violent in action must be that which has the greatest velocity, as its velocity makes its impact most forcible ... If, therefore, the natural constitution of wind is of this kind, it must be the substance whose motive power is the greatest. For even fire when conjoined with wind is blown to flame and moves quickly. So the cause of earth tremors is neither water nor earth but wind, which causes them when the external exhalation flows inwards. (1962: 205)

Yates reports, however, that the quake came 'suddenly' on a clear day: 'No blustering blasts, the weather calm and mild / Good Lord the sudden rareness of the thing / A sudden fear did bring to man and child' (1582: 28). But Harvey, in representing a dispute over natural and supernatural origins of earthquakes, concludes, 'The formal cause [of earthquakes] is nothing but the very manner of this same motion and shaking of the earth without, and the violent kind of striving and wrestling of the winds and exhalations within, which is and must needs be done in this or that sort, after one fashion or other' (Harvey 1580: 11).

Aristotle goes on to analogize the motions of wind in the earth to those within the human body:

> We must suppose, again, that the earth is affected as we often are after making water, when a sort of tremor runs through the body as a body of wind turns inwards again from without. (1962: 209)

While empirical experience had many questioning this explanation for earthquakes, most still assumed the explosive function of wind lay at their root, and the analogy to human digestion remained persuasive to many. We thus have a model in which earthquakes are the warning of God's wrath for presumption, via influences on and motions of the earth, and a model that confuses human and non-human, inside and outside. The explosive force of the earthquake, while comically analogized to human excretory processes, is nevertheless imagined as the voice of God, speaking through His creation to chide human pride and sin.[12] In his analysis of the play, Craig Dionne draws a direct line from stock linguistic constructions like aphorisms, adages and proverbs to the mechanization of human beings via the very thing that is usually cited in distinguishing humans from other forms of life – their use of language. The practice of speaking proverbs 'figures the human subject as a kind of receptacle or automaton who repeats a program written long ago', says Dionne, and argues that *King Lear* is an experiment in 'humanist literacy' that 'dislocate[s] the power of church and state' (2016: 18, 20). Exhalations of the body may not be precisely language itself, but when they are translated by providentialist explanations into evidence of the word of God, they articulate with Dionne's descriptions – they shake up, as it were, traditional forms like proverb or adage, in the interests of resetting the programme.

Whether we see earthquakes as an example of God's dislocating speech or not, generations of critics have seen

Lear's raging on the heath in 3.2 as an example of some connection between King and state, and nature itself. In such readings, Lear's internal tempests reflect and are matched by nature's extreme weather, which blurs, as does an earthquake, inside and outside, human and divine. Indeed, we might even agree that it's possible this terrifying storm within and without Lear is what early moderns would have considered 'earthquake weather'. But this is only a starting point. What would it mean to say that the king's psychic distress manifests in cataclysmic weather patterns? In *Macbeth*, the monarch's death is accompanied by natural phenomena turned unnatural: 'The night has been unruly; where we lay, / Our chimneys were blown down and, as they say, / Lamentings heard in the air ... Some say the earth / Was feverous and did shake' (2.3.54–60). In *A Midsummer Night's Dream*, Titania and Oberon's dispute has resulted in damage to nature's cycles of weather: 'the winds ... have suck'd up from the sea / Contagious fogs; which, falling in the land, / Hath every pelting river made so proud / That they have overborne their continents' (2.1.88–92). Both examples draw a clear line linking rulers and the maintenance of natural order. But in *Lear*, it is the king himself who may have helped generate this quake – Lear's division of his lands via his map, something he imagined to be his prerogative, has effectually riven the kingdom, has become the actual riving of the earth itself. Lear's tempest is not a simple case of nature reflecting the disruption of order; it is the monarch's destruction of order that allows nature to burst free, intruding the unassimilable, ineffable voice of the deity not just to reflect Lear's disrupted analogical connection to the land, but to put into question the value of even a providentialist reading. Mentz points out that 'Providentialism becomes problematic when bad things happen to good people, and the risks of sea travel made Providential control seem both intensely desirable and not entirely comforting' (2015: 6). In Lear's case, we (and Shakespeare's audiences) might wonder if Lear is really bad enough to deserve his punishment, whether his hubris in treating the land as an abstraction justifies his reduction to suffering in bad weather. Are we even supposed to see God's hand in his treatment? Or are we only seeing Lear's *desire* for such an explanation registered in the play's storm? At a minimum, it is difficult to accept that the terrible storms and quakes the characters undergo on the 'heath' show much beyond the inhuman character of Providential utterances, and the hostility of the elements that transmit Providence's counter-programme. If the storm and its quake-like qualities are God's voice, then perhaps God is not someone we want to know.

The 1580 earthquake seems purpose-built as a precursor to Morton's examples of hyperobjects like global warming or radiation. It reminds humans caught up in it of the magnitude of natural elements, the impossibility of a 'god's eye' view of earthquake destruction, and the relative failure of human knowledge to encompass such objects. The play uses blindness, for instance, as the main metaphor for conveying both Lear and Gloucester's incomprehension, their mis-cognition of the world in which both assume they live. But Morton deploys hyperobjects to dispel the idea of a 'world' altogether, in favour of the return of 'the earth', since it is the concept of a world that has prevented our full engagement with ontology, rather than epistemology, where objects are concerned. The world is our blind spot, effacing the earth and its claims on us. Like Lear in his court summoning his map, our conception of a 'world' replaces the matter of the environment with a fable, a fantasy created by humans to articulate human authority and power. To have a *world* is to engage in the creation of a body of knowledge; encountering a hyperobject, on the other hand, prevents the detours epistemology encourages, where denial and affective distance are possible, where human subjectivity is king and the earth merely an object to know (Morton 2013: 5–18). Wandering the material contours of the land it turns out he did not know at all, and battered by the 'fretful elements' (3.1.4), Lear moves just as 'feelingly' as the blind Gloucester, not through a landscape, which might offer a sense of the locality Bradley finds missing in the play, or even with Gloucester's direction (always to Dover), but through one face of the hyperobject that is the earth itself. In other words, Lear encounters an object, discovers his entanglement with its phenomena, and cannot contain the experience either through rational discourse or through its opposite, madness. The play reaches for Providence, and is burned by the touch. What Lear learns instead, I'm arguing, is what it is like to undergo a 'being-quake', a fundamental recalibration of his sensory and intellectual existence. In the final analysis, the land, the earth, the elements that both chafe and feed it, exist without reference to Lear, without consideration of the human at all. Any confidence that critics are right about there being some connection between the weather and Lear's inner state turns out to be merely our own attempt to impose a narrative structure that the earth and its phenomena may not countenance. Readers and audiences, like Lear, are shaken from such certainties. For all Lear's howling at the storm, it neither advances nor retreats because of him, and it does not acknowledge his vocalizations.

Like Lear, Gloucester ends up diminished, revealed in his lame hypocrisy, seeking oblivion. His treatment at his son Edgar's hands can perplex both students and critics of the play: why bother to lead this suffering old man toward Dover's cliffs, where he hopes to do away with himself, allowing him to remain convinced both sons have abandoned him? Why set up the theatre of his approach to the cliff's edge, and allow him to 'jump'? I'm going to posit that part of the answer lies in both the reports of the 1580 earthquake, and in Gloucester's own refrain as he moves across the land's inhospitable surface. Tarleton's account highlights a series of stories about the earthquake's effects:

> Two or three honest men that walked for their pleasure into Moorfeeld (sitting upon a hill) *were upon a sudden tumbled down* with such violence that when they recovered themselves: they were so amazed that for a good space *they could not one speak* to the other.

> Two honest Men more sitting on a Cannon upon Tower hill were *on a sudden thrown off* and the Cannons rolled and hopped up and down very strange.
>
> The very waters and ditches shook and frothed wonderfully. (Campbell 1941: 298 italics added)

Of course people fall down during earthquakes, nothing surprising there. But as Laurie Shannon has pointed out, the precariousness of human balance in locomotion figures in early modern disputes over the reason and significance of bipedalism: on the one hand, writers opine that human uprightness is a sign of mankind's focus on, and relation to heaven; on the other, human bipedalism must be acknowledged inferior to quadripedalism because it renders humans more vulnerable to stumbling, tripping and other accidents in encounters with the earth beneath their feet.[13] Earthquakes remind humans of their inadequacy in the face of massive shocks to the environment; they also remind humans that they are subject to the insecurities of their own physiological structure. As much as earthquakes, especially the 1580 one, are noted for toppling church steeples, they are equally noted for rendering humans prostrate, upending them, turning them fleetingly (if we take Tarleton's account as a template) into speechless toys surrounded by temporarily animate fellow objects like cannons and ditches. Gloucester's 'being-quake' prompts his recognition that his upright posture is not a given, and not attached to any superior moral or intellectual capacity: 'I have no way and therefore want no eyes; / I stumbled when I saw' (4.1.18–19).

'Let him smell his way to Dover', says Regan (3.6.96–7), and indeed Gloucester doggedly persists on that route: 'Know'st thou the way to Dover', he asks Poor Tom, and again, 'Dost thou know Dover?' (4.1.54, 70). *Knowing* Dover: unlike the Gloucester, or the Lear, of the play's opening, there are no maps, no letters, no courtly humanist accoutrements to guide the old man, only bodily smelling and feeling and the aid of similarly reduced figures like the Old Man and Poor Tom.

Knowing, I'm arguing, is precisely what the being-quakes of the play undo. Only by 'un-knowing', by emerging from the 'world' of epistemological certainties conferred by humanist knowledge, do Gloucester and Lear manage a partial return from the depths of their alienation in the wild weather of the heath, or on the 'high and bending head' of Dover's cliffs.[14] Bipedal, reasoning, educated, and social humankind's fate when faced with cosmological forces like earthquakes, or the being-quakes the play associates with them, is to stumble and be pitched headlong – except, as Gloucester discovers, once he embraces such an outcome he falls onto level land and is reunited with his loyal son:

> GLOUCESTER [KNEELING]
>   O you mighty gods! This world do I renounce, and in
>   your sights
>   Shake patiently my great affliction off.
>   If I could bear it any longer and not fall
>   To quarrel with your great opposeless wills,
>   My snuff and loathed part of nature should
>   Burn itself out. If Edgar live, oh bless him!
>   Now, fellow, fare thee well. [*he falls*]
>   (4.6.34–41)

Uncertain what has happened, he asks 'But have I fall'n or no?' Both Gloucester's sentiments about the gods' 'opposeless wills', and his uncertainty in his own knowledge ('have I fall'n?') – if not, granted, his suicide attempt – would have warmed the hearts of the earthquake pamphleteers and poets. Kneeling and falling are stages on the way to full restoration of his mind and family; the earthquake has produced its inevitable result, and, like the storm on the heath, reduced Gloucester to the humility of un-knowing.

Is this Mentz's idea of shipwreck's 'salvage', or drying out after surviving the catastrophe?[15] Or is it the irredeemable tragedy of the play that knowledge fails and unknowing cannot save the 'human' from suffering and the operation of indifferent forces like the weather, the stars or fate? The former is posthumanist, the latter humanist. Should we call Lear's cosmos Christian and apocalyptic? Or might we profitably read it as presaging a cosmos based on a ruthless kind of Darwinian evolution, in which the weak and old are cleared away and the unsuccessful mutations killed off? Both of these views could be considered humanist, yet the Darwinian cosmos has posthumanist potential: one could argue that in order for recovery to occur and life to continue the play requires the erasure of the epistemologically presumptuous older generation and their victims – including of course Cordelia, but also, however much we might hate to say they might belong to a redemptive futurity, Cornwall, Regan, Goneril and Edmund, all of whom have invested in variations of the model of 'the world' Lear and Gloucester constructed. Lear's last speech complains that 'a dog, a horse, a rat' (5.3.312) all have life when his daughter does not, reminding us, perhaps perversely, that life *does* go on. Only it's not the anthropocentric or egotistical version of life that obtained throughout the majority of the play. 'O you mighty gods!' Gloucester apostrophizes, assuming a posture of abjection and blind acceptance. 'We must obey', says Edgar, summing up the play – but it isn't God he means to obey, but 'the weight of this sad time' (5.3.331). How does one obey a weight, or time? I'm tempted to speculate on the hint of some notion of gravity's pull in Edgar's final words, 'we that are young / Shall never see so much nor live so long' (5.3.332), registering that humanity is never fully 'upright', or capable of rising aspirationally. Nor does God seem to be at the root of human suffering in this moment; rather, forces beyond even religion's ability to comprehend bear down on us all. Edgar reaches for the proverbial, which Dionne would argue can provide comfort and possible transmission of truths; and he invokes something that is almost, but not quite Providential, which would restore a divine dimension to the cosmos. But neither cosmological organizing principle is quite *there* any longer, and neither is adequate to the task of restoring the 'gored state' (5.3.326). Instead, Edgar proposes a decline, the vitiation of offspring, the shortening of life and the limiting of vision. Survivors may adapt, but in losing faith in the cosmological makeup of the past, they are reduced. My reading here does not, as many critics have done, see the flight of hope in humanist terms. Instead, it embraces the play's posthumanist potential, emphasizing that the aftershock of Lear's death involves an acknowledgement of human insignificance, incoherence and decline, that is not reassimilated to any ponderous humanist framework of interpretation.

3

Bodies and Minds

Julie Taymor's 1999 film *Titus* offers audiences the indelible image of a raped and mutilated Lavinia, discovered by her uncle Marcus holding out arms that are bloodily severed at the wrists, and to which are somehow bound bundles of leafless branches. Not only does the image make concrete Shakespeare's reference in *Titus Andronicus* to the 'branches' of the Andronici family that have been 'lopped' by her violation, but it provides the justification, metaphorical and material, for a second strange addition on Taymor's part: in the film, young Lucius arranges to give a carved wooden prosthetic hand to his maimed aunt, presumably presenting her with a more 'life-like' replacement for those wooden branches. He selects a delicate version that he finds in a workshop full of disembodied human legs, feet, hands, arms and other body parts.

Taymor's Lavinia is thus re-introduced to her family after her trauma at the hands of Chiron and Demetrius as a wounded body capable of being supplemented (if not restored) by both nature and human ingenuity. Through the devices of branches and prosthetics, Taymor makes visible and tangible the variety of registers in which the play marks Lavinia's disability. Shorn of her hands and tongue, two unique signs of human exceptionalism in much early modern writing because of their connection to language and material creativity, Lavinia is not merely sexually violated, but doubly silenced, denied speech *and* writing.[1] Marcus deems her abuser 'a craftier Tereus' (2.4.40) who has made her less 'effectual' than the mythic Philomel, unable even to weave the story of her rape in a tapestry. The 'delightful engine' that was her tongue has joined her 'handless' condition (3.1.82, 67) and reduced her to a series of confusions and substitutions.[2] The play forces on its audience an uncomfortable awareness of what Lavinia lacks, and how that lack can be filled: Marcus offers her his staff to hold in her mouth and write the names of her attackers in the sand, while Titus has her take his own severed hand in her mouth. Even when she holds the basin for the Goths' blood in her 'stumps' (5.2.182), a kind of exchange takes place, of their 'guilty blood' (5.2.183) for the innocent blood shed during her mutilation. Of course, the hole that can't be made 'whole' by filling or supplementing is the unseen one involved in her loss of chastity, according to Titus 'more dear / Than hands or tongue' (5.2.175–6).

The play's disabling of Lavinia, and her gradual reconstruction as an assemblage of natural and manufactured objects that can manipulate wood, sand and blood to satisfy Titus's need for revenge, resonates with many similar instances in Shakespeare's work in which characters confront what we would now call bodily 'disability'. Most often, scholars of the period interested in disability studies focus on obvious examples like hunchbacked Richard III, the *Tempest*'s fishman Caliban, or 'deformed' Thersites in *Troilus and Cressida*; but as David Houston Wood points out, the list of characters with 'variant' bodies is immensely long (from blinded Gloucester in *King Lear* to Katharina's limp in *Taming of the Shrew*, from Othello's epilepsy to fat Falstaff in the histories and *The Merry Wives of Windsor*), inviting audiences and readers to consider the ways Shakespeare 'assays and delimits the human' (Wood 2016: 193). Indeed, Wood challenges us to see disability in so many forms and places, including women's barrenness, drunkenness, bastardy and old age, in order to suggest that compromised characters might easily be counted a norm, rather than a departure from some ordinary standard of ablebodiedness. Vin Nardizzi argues that even locating disability only in the body fails to 'capture the full meaning of 'disability' in the early modern period' (2016: 456). Further, many such characters are deployed to chart the negative against which 'whole' individuals can be recognized by contrast, as if the category of humans defined as able-bodied is an empty one, constructed only through examples of what it is not.[3] Such a process would require the constant discovery of disability, its constant reproduction, revealing both ability and disability to be constructed, not inherent.

There are many other ways, and other domains in which to think about bodily disability. Caroline Lamb, for example, argues that Shakespeare's *Titus Andronicus* depicts characters undergoing 'loss, fragmentation and trauma' not merely to tell a story about decline and dissolution; rather, Titus and Lavinia, like Rome itself, recuperate, adapt, and find new forms of integrated or organic wholeness (2010: 43). As Lamb notes, the analogy that insistently compares the state to a body, with diverse operations assigned to specific organs and dependent on a ruling 'head' to control its passions, underwrites early modern political theory and is ubiquitous in Shakespeare's plays.[4] The analogy can be adapted to highlight the threat of trade, or of incursions of foreigners (see for instance, Harris 1998), or used to quell rebellion as it is in the opening scene of *Coriolanus* (Höfele 2011; Pfannebecker 2012). The analogy functions in *Titus Andronicus* to mark both Saturninus and the Goths as pathological elements that destabilize Rome, throwing its body politic into chaos. The Goths' actions, however, are predicated on Titus's choices, indicating that the Roman 'body' was never as cohesive or healthy as it imagined, given its wanton sacrifice of its children to war. And by the play's conclusion, just what kind of entitlement an able body confers on its possessor is unclear. Titus's loss of a hand through Aaron's stratagem in Act 3 is only one manifestation of the truncating and impoverishing values that his service to the state long ago instilled in his intact, martial body. The citizens' appeal to make Titus their emperor may seem a celebration of his able-bodied entitlement, but his murder of his son Mutius (who should be seen as an extension of his and Rome's body and being) is an equally direct result, and constitutes a kind of self-murder, a sign of Titus's dis-ease following years of war. Strong, weak, healthy, or compromised, nearly all of the play's characters end up pierced, wounded, minced, eaten, dying or dead.

Posthumanist theory is necessarily concerned with both human bodies and human minds, especially with the way philosophical and cultural characterizations of both have been wielded in the interests of human exceptionalism and humanist hubris, and so posthumanist theory can be understood as generatively inclusive with regard to disability theory.[5] As we have seen in the work of Katherine Hayles, summarized in the introduction, the place of the body in current technocentric accounts of the posthuman is vexed. The idea that consciousness cannot be divided from the biological substrate that is the body can disrupt liberal humanism's version of the self, of humanist subjectivity; but it can also reassert a humanist anthropocentrism of thought and practice (Wolfe 2010: xxiii–xxv). For Hayles, there is no consciousness without the processes, engagements and interrelations of bodies with environments, and no 'mind' without the brain and the body. Other critics and scholars who would identify as posthumanist have addressed the role of the Enlightenment version of embodiment in establishing a narrowly heteronormative sexuality (Grosz 1994) or mobilizing bodies in the interests of capitalist economics (see for instance, Braidotti 2013: 57–67). Yet however salutary many challenges to Enlightenment body/mind dualism might be, by taking that binary as their point of departure they run the risk of making that Enlightenment version of embodiment seem natural and inevitable rather than fully historically contingent.

Studies of the early modern body dating back to the 1980s have emphasized the porous and unstable nature of bodily identity in pre-Enlightenment historical context. Against modern ideas about the body as a solid, closed container, a *homo clausus* or enclosed individual, with impassable, defensible and rigidly drawn boundaries, early modern scholars have posited the historical role of humoralism and the passions in constructing bodies that were open to their environments – sometimes uncomfortably, sometimes joyfully – as well as subject to the fluidity of their own internal processes. In other words, the deconstructed 'posthuman' body and embodied mind Hayles and other theorists are proposing was in many ways an ordinary experience for early moderns.

Yet this 'passible' (Paster 2016: 178) body has nonetheless continued in many ways to be understood as a mostly intact, biological and ontologically coherent entity. Scholars interested in disability studies have countered with the insight that 'able' and 'disabled' are 'elastic social categor[ies] both subject to social control and capable of effecting social change' (Siebers 2008). Wood and Lamb, along with Nardizzi (2012, 2016), Allison Hobgood (2009) and Hobgood and Wood (2013) and a growing number of other scholars have addressed questions about how these categories are established, disseminated or interrogated on the early modern stage. Returning to the pre-Enlightenment moment of Shakespeare's plays might allow us to imagine the dominance of the Enlightenment body/self dyad as neither natural nor inevitable. In relation to disability studies, this move is especially potentially fruitful: modern concepts and definitions of disability attempt to undo the category of 'able' in much the same way that posthumanism undoes the category of 'the human' – so human is revealed to be a null category, a continually manufactured division that is fictional in origin, variable and unstable, and finally always compromised and incomplete. Early modern literature, which has not yet subscribed to the absolute binaries or dichotomies, whether between human and animal as we shall see in Chapter 4, or body and mind as this chapter details, grants us postmoderns the opportunity to think about alternative positions outside of, or qualifying, such binaries. Likewise, Shakespeare's plays hint that there is as yet in his world no such thing as the fully realized 'able' body; there are certainly premonitions of it in humanist discourse and cultural artefacts (think for example of da Vinci's idealized Vitruvian Man or

Pico's transcendent humanist subject), but these concepts are as yet infirm, embryonic or inconsistent. Where no automatic assumption of a fully 'able' body obtains, the process by which able/disabled is constructed and legitimized can be more readily observed.

Equally, the perception that, as Lennard Davis argues, disability is not so much a subcategory of identity as it is a universal state of being is an experiential fact for early modernity. Arguing for what he calls 'dismodernism', Davis points out that the very concerns expressed by those resisting the expansion of disability rights – that too many kinds of things now count as disability – is in fact an insight into modernity's destabilization of essential categories of identity. It is 'the postmodern subject position', full stop (2002: 14), and allows for 'a commonality of bodies within the notion of difference' (31). Davis does not discount the role of identity in grounding resistance to oppression, but makes the case that history, science, theory and experience have converged to make it necessary to rethink identity and its consequences; disability's 'inherently unstable' definition and its 'very difference from traditional identities, its malleable and shaky foundation' (5) can aid in what is in many ways a posthumanist agenda. Disability may not even necessarily be a minority attribute in a world that has pierced the genetic code, that has invented devices of war that can lash out well beyond their immediate time of use, and in which populations live long enough to widely exhibit the diminished capacities of old age. Shakespeare's England did not possess the technologies (like implants or mechanical and synthetic replacements for skin, bone, blood vessels, teeth, hair, hearing or vision) the ubiquity of which can complicate the postmodern body's 'able' status into sheer incoherence, but as Wood's long list of variously impaired characters in the plays hints, Davis's claim that 'what is universal in life ... is the experience of the limitation of the body' (32) would have been indisputably true for premoderns. What's more, that view was incorporated into the most deeply held belief systems of Shakespeare's time: Christianity did not merely hold the body to be a sink of sin, a drag on the spirit or a reminder of the flesh's mortality, but insisted on the body's failings as a reminder of humanity's uniform *dependence* on God's grace. John Donne saw the fear his physician roused in him as salutary for giving him insight: 'My weaknesse', he wrote of that fear, 'is from Nature, who hath but her Measure, my strength is from God, who possesses, and distributes infinitely' (1959: 36). Human beings might imagine themselves superior creatures, upright and therefore closer to heaven; but Donne asks

> what state hath he in this dignitie? A fever can fillip him downe, a fever can depose him; a fever can bring that head, which yesterday carried a crown of gold, five foot towards a crown of glory, as low as his own foot, today. When God came to breathe into Man the breath of life, he found him flat upon the ground; when he comes to withdraw that breath from him again, he prepares him to it, by laying him flat upon his bed. (17)

For Donne, as for many devoutly religious early moderns, human beings were all compromised in body as in soul, and whatever 'ability' they were granted was fleeting and nothing to be smug about. To be assaulted in body or mind could even be viewed as a blessing, since the link between the wounded human body and Christ's wounds on the cross was a common theme in religious iconography and meditation.[6]

In this chapter, I account for the history of scholarship on early modern embodiment and consciousness, and for its recent encounters with critics interested in disability studies. I then offer a brief reading of the place where body and mind most clearly intersect: the face. My discussion touches on debates in philosophy and theory over the place of the face as the source of intersubjective ethical relations. However, I read Shakespeare's plays as staging a fundamental problem with the material fact of having a face. It is not merely that, as Duncan famously puts it in *Macbeth*, there's no definitive art to find 'the mind's construction in the face' (*Macbeth* 1.4.13–14). Faces and visages promise readability, promise a direct and meaningful relation between inside and outside, between mind and body. Indeed, early modern phrenology constituted an attempt to found a science in that correspondence (Baumbach 2008). But as Duncan and others in Shakespeare's plays discover, faces conceal as much as reveal – and they are themselves mere assemblages of parts, prosthetic in only partial and inconsistent ways to each other and to the minds they are presumed to represent in the world. In face-to-face encounters, Shakespeare's humans thus experience a primal array of dis-abilities: some, like Duncan, cannot read faces, but others cannot put their own faces together, and still other characters find that faces migrate from human Others to other Others – to entirely non-human objects and phenomena. Perhaps paradoxically or ironically, the neurological process by which such an experience is made possible, *pareidolia* or the brain's tendency to find faces in non-human objects or visual representations, now perplexes scientists who dispute whether it is a specifically human trait, or whether it might be something of which all animate creatures' brains (perhaps even their 'minds') are capable. Regardless of the answer to that conundrum, pareidolia is a hint that the outward apparatus that is the human face stabilizes nothing related to either being or behaviour. Concluding the chapter, Shakespeare's *Love's Labour's Lost* provides a proving ground for these and more insights about posthumanism and the face.

Bodies

Shakespeare's plays frequently recognize the body's vulnerability both to assaults from without and to disruptions within. Bodily integrity can be violated of course by injuries or scars, or threatened by dissolution, disease and death. But it also undergoes a constant onslaught from less obvious sources. Gail Kern Paster's important work on humoralism and embodiment in the period has restored our sense that even the most 'able' early modern body was always battered by internal and external imbalances (1993). Humoralism was the medical theory inherited from Galen that viewed the human body as containing four 'humours' or elements – black and yellow bile, blood and phlegm. Such a simple configuration, however, misrepresents what was a highly complex and evolved way of thinking not just about what was in the body, but what influenced it from outside. Bodies were, for instance, additionally understood to be hot or cold by virtue of sex, and their internal balances upset or restored by types of food, quality and temperature of air and region, quantity of fluids consumed, activities engaged in and so on. Thus, an ideal balance of humours that could guarantee health was extremely difficult to achieve. Regimes of diet, advice on travel or relocation, remedies for everything from specific ailments to overall sexual health, and many other aspects of daily life were all tied to an understanding of an individual's humoral makeup. What's more, humoralism connected mental and emotional states to this material system, so that, as Paster notes, early moderns experienced both their social and individual identities as the byproduct of physical, humoral balances (1993: 7). Her work focuses on the gender and class implications of having particular kinds of humoral bodies – what Norbert Elias called 'the civilizing process' required increasing 'regulation of a subject's experience of his/her own body and relations with the bodies of others' (164). Women, for instance, were viewed as 'leaky vessels', moist and cold, but less capable of self-governance because of their bodies' ungoverned intake and excretions (in blood, urine and faeces). Caesar's grotesque body is revealed as subject to similarly 'womanly incontinence' (Paster 1993: 94) when it bleeds indiscriminately, while lower-class bodies are equally grotesque in their association with uncontrolled excretions of other kinds. Michael Schoenfeldt has additionally argued that the humoral body and its necessary regulation could contribute to an emerging proto-modern sense of interiority, an affirmation of the existence of the 'self' articulated in literature through a 'poetics of corporeal experience' (1999: 171). Body and soul, body and character, body and emotion were thus always 'fully imbricated' (Schoenfeldt 1999: 1). Schoenfeldt argues that early moderns viewed the ideal body as a space of orderly flows; thus temperance or careful restraint is the quintessential virtue of a Galenic humoral system.

Paster's and Schoenfeldt's arguments do not always align, suggesting that early modern thought about the body was varied in its origins and therefore also often conflicted. David Hillman in turn only adds to the possible divergent lines of thought about early modern embodiment when he argues in *Shakespeare's Entrails* (2007) that out of the confusion of differing attitudes and conceptions of the body we can find hints of a certain process of enclosure, of withdrawal from the environment, and the first hints of a disembodied subject that will become the *homo clausus* of the later seventeenth and eighteenth centuries. Hillman sees in Shakespeare's work signs that the porous, open body was already a thing of the past, and so departs from both Paster and Schoenfeldt. For all three, however, what is crucial are the correspondences and coincidences of what postmoderns would think of as distinct kinds of experience – mental, psychological, religious and physiological, or in simpler terms, material and (apparently) immaterial. We can also see in all these lines of inquiry a common sense that the early modern body was at significant points in its conceptualization indistinct from its environment, what Stacy Alaimo would call transcorporeal, subject to the agential influences of other kinds of matter (2010). Alaimo dismantles the modern *homo clausus* from a presentist posthumanist ecocritical perspective, but her descriptions of bodies that are penetrable, bodies for which the pretence of singularity and control is always under erasure in the face of external forces would have sounded familiar to most early moderns. In Alaimo's work, environmental matter can change human anatomy and human psychology;[7] bodies are not merely discursively constructed, and do not simply precede their material relations with their environments. Human and non-human are open to one another, constitute one another; the human is not therefore an absolute, a pre-existing condition of being.

For early moderns, sensory messages were complexly linked to issues of bodily and spiritual integrity. A whole literature of sensation has arisen in scholarship on the period: Carla Mazzio (2003) and Joe Moshenska (2014) on touch, Bruce R. Smith on sound (1999), Holly Dugan on smell (2011), and a number of other emerging voices add to an already extensive representation of visual regimes in the period.[8] Some senses provoke anxiety over the body's ability to defend itself against incursion; others help the body navigate the world. Yet all sensory engagements with the exterior of the body accomplish more than either of these options can summarize. Indeed, as much as humoral theory defined the body's experience of ingress and egress via the digestive system, placing it at the centre of the discourse on bodies in the same way that the stomach rests at the centre of the body itself (Hillman 2007) tends to relegate the senses to some idea of a periphery; this is exactly wrong. Sensory enmeshment in an environment is the broader and more absolute condition of bodily being (and, as we will see, of mental existence). Shakespeare's characters encounter their worlds through sensory inputs, often confusing or confused synaesthetic experiences, and are constructed through their relation to those inputs. Sensory experience can have political, cultural, religious or other kinds of social implications; it also, however, always constitutes the bodies at the core of those implications. Duke Orsino in *Twelfth Night* gives a famous synaesthetic speech collapsing taste and sound: 'If music be the food of love, play on; / Give me excess of it, that surfeiting, / The appetite may sicken and die. / That strain again, it had a dying fall; / O it came o'er my ear like the sweet sound / That breathes upon a bank of violets / Stealing and giving odor' (1.1.1–7). Here, Orsino describes music in terms of both taste and smell, as if each sense were inadequate to fully express the strength of his desire for 'sweet sound' to accompany his languishing longing for Olivia. In the same way that Orsino collapses one kind of desire with another regarding music, he also conflates infatuation with love, will with virtue, jealousy with sexual passion, and imagination with reality. In her analysis of the play's puns and allusions, Frances Dolan explores the many possible connections between Orsino's references to music and violets, which proleptically echo Viola's name and her role as musician (playing, perhaps, a viol de gamba) when dressed as Cesario (Dolan 2014: 49). But at the same time, Orsino's confused synaesthetic paean announces his own simultaneous egoism and utter loss of identity – as a duke, his passive state is untoward, while sensorially he is cut off from all other forms of encounter with the social and natural world. In effect, Orsino has his earbuds in and refuses to converse sensibly with his fellows or partake in healthy and robustly aristocratic male activities (when Curio asks if he'll go hunt, he refuses with a speech that goes wandering off into obscure – and dangerously violent – allusions to hearts/harts and Actaeon's death from attack by his own hounds). His surfeited sensorium is both a physiological state, and an allegory for Orsino's current psychology. In both those dimensions he fails not through a deficit, but through excess and access.

Other examples of the confusion of bodily senses and environments abound. Macbeth's castle, for instance, is perversely pleasing to Duncan and Banquo, leading the latter to comment that 'heaven's breath smells wooingly' there. Pestilential air contaminates it once Duncan is no more. Jonathan Gil Harris describes the 'olfactory palimpsest' that defines *Macbeth* as a 'subject's polychronic experience of an object' (2008: 124) where the thing that smells is at once itself, and evocative of associations in the memory of the smelling subject. Theatrical use of squibs during performances of *Macbeth* to produce effects of thunder and lightning would have bathed the Globe in sulphurous odours. The resulting 'olfactory confusion' (Harris 2008: 132) as much as it shaped the internal political world of the play defined the audience's experience of *Macbeth* in part by eliciting memories of the historical Gunpowder Plot. Political disruption, the confusion of religious identity, and the consequent violation of a quasi-sacred space during an attempt on the king's life aligned momentarily with the horror of witnessing a fictional regicide in progress on stage. Only the senses could produce this layering of memory, identity and meaning.

In Bruce Smith's work, sound is the focus of what he calls 'historical phenomenology' (1999: 22), detailing the 'soundscapes' in which early moderns dwelt and which shaped their experience of life and art. The Globe created a complex sound environment within what was the shockingly cacophonous urban environment of London. In 1613 the Globe burned to the ground after an accident involving cannon fire as part of a performance of *All Is True*, a play about Henry VIII. Imagine for a moment what the sound of such cannon, even if somehow dampened for the location, would have been like in an enclosed space; apparently to those at the play, it was not so loud as to be unbearable, which makes sense if we consider Smith's description of London's excessive general decibel level. We generally think of the more salutary sounds of Shakespeare's plays, the beautiful songs, the music, the poetry of many speeches. Yet these were released into a space occupied by breathing, probably stinking, chattering, eating, rustling, coughing, sweating, spitting, perhaps laughing or weeping people, over the massed noise and odour of whom much of the impact of these subtle elements would have struggled to emerge.[9]

Much Ado About Nothing relies on multiple confusions, of sight, sound and words (Henderson 2010: 193) – masked balls, mistaken identities, misunderstood speeches, mistaken textual evidence, that are only put right by the efforts of a garbled, impaired constabulary. *A Midsummer Night's Dream* gives us Bottom, who exhibits the same verbal indeterminacy as *Much Ado*'s Dogberry in his mangled rendering of I Corinthians upon waking from his enchantment: 'The eye of man hath not heard, the ear of man hath not seen, man's hand is not able to taste, his tongue to conceive, nor hisheart to report what my dream was' (4.1.202–10). Even as Pyramus, Bottom cannot sort the senses from one another: 'I see a voice. Now will I to the chink / To spy an I can hear my Thisbe's face' (5.1.191–2).[10] It might be tempting to throw Dogberry and Bottom in one basket and associate their inability – their disability – regarding organized bodily experience with their class; but Orsino and others prove this is incorrect. Rather, all characters seem submerged in differing degrees of chaos. No surprise then that so many plays dwell on the confusion of senses, via synaesthesia, or the disconcerting awareness characters develop of their porous, and therefore vulnerable relation to the world around them.

Minds

We've seen that some forms of what we now consider mental functioning (psychology; morality; spirituality) were for Shakespeare's world indivisible from the bodies that experienced that world through their senses or in terms of their presumed humoral balances. Recent scholarship also makes the case that the mental world of Shakespeare's characters is a textbook example of what is sometimes called 'cognitive ecology', the association of all levels and types of mental or psychological phenomena with the interaction of body and environment. Countering the Cartesian dualism that divides a unitary, individuated 'mind' from the body and world it supposedly inhabits, as if reason occurred independently of and without reference to information gleaned by means of physical encounters, cognitive ecology generally asserts that such a picture is entirely inaccurate. For instance, Humberto Maturana and Francisco Varela's work on the embodied mind undoes the premise that there is such a thing as a transcendental 'I' that thinks and acts as the vessel of memory and experience (Maturana and Varela 1980; Varela, Thompson and Rosch 1991). George Lakoff and Mark Johnson assert that cognitive science has answered the questions that Western philosophy has speculated about for a century, and those answers undo philosophy's dualism and its definitions of reason: 'Our most basic philosophical beliefs are tied inextricably to our view of reason. Reason has been taken for over two millennia as the defining characteristic of human beings ... A radical change in our understanding of reason is therefore a radical change in our understanding of ourselves' (1999: 3). Reason, they go on to explain, 'arises from the nature of our brains, bodies, and bodily experience. This is not just the innocuous and obvious claim that we need a body to reason; rather, it is the striking claim that the very structure of reason itself comes from the details of our embodiment' (4).

If there is no transcendental I, and if reason is determined by embodiment, then notions of subjective experience, of subjectivity itself undergo thorough revision. Human selves, even those discursively constituted, have a certain claim to agency and self-consciousness; the self is a unique entity that presumes to act via the exertion of will in and on the world. Descartes located subjectivity in thought itself; Kant's *Critique of Pure Reason* asserted that the subject required objects (that is, the mind requires a reality in which to act) to exist at all – but the mind shapes experience. Subsequent philosophical arguments qualified the subject's nature and structure, until Freud and Marx exposed the limits of the subject's knowledge and control: both questioned the subject's unitary and autonomous nature, Freud from the perspective of the workings of the unconscious, and Marx from the perspective of ideology's ability to construct a false sense of reality (see Badmington 2000: 4–9). Anti-humanist thought throughout the second half of the twentieth century continued to put pressure on the subject by describing it as the byproduct of material or semiotic systems. Yet some version of the subject as an organizing entity, along with the subject's association with reason (even if corrupted and false) and self-identity (even if not fully conscious of the forces that bring it into being), remains intact through these historical-philosophical movements.[11]

Lakoff and Johnson chart the ways these versions of reason and the subject are undermined by neuroscience's discoveries: there is no autonomous rational person who exercises free will, as Kant would claim; there is equally, however, no economic subject who makes rational choices to 'maximize utility' and no 'phenomenological person, who through phenomenological introspection alone can discover everything there is to know about our mind and the nature of experience' (1999: 5). Perhaps more radically, Lakoff and Johnson *do* assert a universality but one involving evolution's influence on bodies to ensure that our conceptual systems are held in common; thus for them post-structuralism is also wrong in its embrace of relativism, fragmentation and historical contingency. Although they assert something they repeatedly call a 'human being' in their work, Lakoff and Johnson's 'human', like Varela and Maturana's, does not validate any kind of Enlightenment humanism, or even resemble our usual anthropocentric version of 'the human' – their 'human' is only a distinct kind of animal with a particular evolutionary history that does not entitle it to any special ontological status. It thus implicitly articulates with posthumanist dismantling of 'the human'.

Like embodied cognition, embedded forms of cognition dismantle the presumptions of Enlightenment philosophy of mind and consciousness, only with different results. Embedded cognition includes theories of distributed or extended mind that focus on the means by which mental processes are offloaded to social, cultural, or physical environments. Theories of distributed cognition or the extended mind, for example, demonstrate the way what we think of as the mind's work in terms of memory, analysis, reason and so on can involve a number of diverse partners. Andy Clark and David Chalmers in their foundational 1998 study 'The Extended Mind', cite examples involving the use of mnemonic devices like notes, which function not just as additions or supplements to the mind's ability, but as part of the 'actively externalized' structure of memory itself (10). A more familiar and current example would be the smart phone that gives its user access to a huge range of information and triggers for memory; probably most of us would agree that more than just giving us another tool for thinking about, remembering or knowing things, smart phones change the *structure* of our thinking and redefine what it is possible for us to think. We no longer need to keep facts in mind through memorization, when we have them at our fingertips; we no longer assume that finding information or communicating with others will even involve the process of writing or reading, when we can instantly send video, gifs, images and emojis. Deciphering a map and gaining a sense of orientation in a new place, or even overall, is no longer essential when a voice can tell us what turn to take and when to arrive at a destination. The implications of such devices are profound: instead of a mind that stops, as Clark and Chalmers put it, at the limit of skin and skull, that is within the body and delimited by it, the extended mind exists in a reciprocal, coupled system where the external device is not passive, but an active part of the cognitive process. 'If we remove the external component the system's behavioral competence will drop, just as it would if we removed part of its brain' (1998: 11–12) write Clark and Chalmers, describing nearly every smart phone user's experience of being somehow intellectually diminished when that phone goes missing. Even abstract concepts or beliefs can have an external component, ultimately deconstructing the boundaries that separate the conscious, thinking, believing, self from its environment.

Scholars have brought embodied and extended mind theories to bear on Shakespeare's plays, and on the conditions of the early modern theatre that produced them. In *Cognition in the Globe* (2011), Evelyn Tribble describes the way props, stage architecture, posted manuscript lists, musical cues and the embodied skills of other actors, as elements of a distributed mind that allowed actors at the Globe Theatre to deal with the enormous mnemonic burden involved in successfully performing a number of plays almost daily. Amy Cook's *Shakespearean Neuroplay* (2010) takes up *Hamlet*, the play that most often crystallizes humanist arguments about Shakespeare's thought and influence, and reads its use of mirrors and mirroring through several chapters. Cook's argument concludes with a consideration of how Renaissance views on the skills of acting anticipate the discovery of mirror neurons, neurons that fire both when a body acts and when it perceives another acting (thereby making mimicry and imitation a fundamental structural part of human cognition). Miranda Anderson returns to the mirror in her *Renaissance Extended Mind* (2015), which traces evidence and forms of extended mind in Shakespeare's plays, and suggests that because early moderns connected what we have come to think of as a purely material process in terms of God and the soul, they were especially fascinated by the effects of that process. Shakespeare's Sonnet 77, for instance, which begins by naming the beloved boy's 'glass' where his fading beauty will be reflected, advises the use of a memorandum book that can restore memory:

> Look what thy memory cannot contain,
> Commit to these waste blanks, and thou shalt find
> Those children nursed, delivered from thy brain,
> To take a new acquaintance of thy mind.
> These offices, so oft as thou wilt look,
> Shall profit thee and much enrich thy book.

The poem establishes, Anderson points out, a circular process by which the 'limited and leaky' mind is supplemented by a more durable object, the book, which is therefore both like and unlike memory itself (it can hold memories like the mind, but is less ephemeral); this also implicates writer and book in a mutual process of creation, in which the writer is reproduced in (and as the poem has suggested, will synaesthetically 'taste' the 'learning' provided by) his own thoughts, made physically present in the written text (Anderson 2015: 236–41).

Although theories of embodied cognition and extended mind are not always identified explicitly with posthumanism in such scholarship, when incorporated into approaches to

Shakespeare's plays they do establish a resonance between early modern concerns with minds and bodies, and posthumanist agendas. Neuroscience need not be inherently posthumanist, but it has certainly taken steps toward dethroning the imperial human subject and breaking down the mind's presumed separateness and transcendence of the body and the world. If we bring together the scholarship on humoralism with that concerned with the distributed and extended mind, we arrive at a version of 'the human' in Shakespeare's plays that seems recognizably posthuman *and* posthumanist. How characters think, what they think about, when and why they think, and who they are because of those thoughts are all determined not by some abstraction we could call a 'mind', or even by the brain housed in their skulls, but by humours, sensory inputs, climate, preferred activities, not to mention gender, race, nation and ethnicity – and prostheses of all kinds. Here, the issue of disability's role in these plays again arises. Think once more of *Titus Andronicus*'s Lavinia, with her severed hands and tongue. She is at once absolutely inhuman, cut off from the instruments that early modernity saw as fundamental to the distinction that set human beings off from all other creatures; and at the same time, she could arguably be said to represent both the most ubiquitous premodern version of embodiment, *and* the posthuman condition, since both are characterized by penetrability and prosthetic supplementation, by distributing communication (or an expression of 'mind') across other people or instruments. We needn't only think of Lavinia remedying her dehumanized state through Lucius's book and Marcus's staff; instead we might think of her becoming an embodied exemplar of the para-human status of both bodies and minds.[12] Both Titus and Marcus assume an interiority for Lavinia, but they do so by projecting their own reactions onto her bodily signals. 'Shall I speak for thee' asks the horrified Marcus when he discovers her bleeding: but he has already done so, interpreting her blush and attempt to hide herself as 'shame' (2.4.33; 28). 'I can interpret all her martyred signs', says Titus later, 'She says she drinks no other drink but tears / Brewed with her sorrow, mashed upon her cheeks' (3.2.36–8). Jennifer Munroe has argued that these moments indicate the dangers of 'speaking for' both women and nature, for substituting the voices of the same for moments of difference, even inscrutable difference. For Munroe, the supplanting of female voice by male speech is paralleled in the damage that occurs when human perspectives substitute for and distort non-human needs, experiences or contexts. But I would add that humans never actually quite speak for themselves in any case: the meaning of speech is always mediated, delegated, alienated, whether through blushes, gestures, books, writing, the shape of tongue and teeth, by the memory of words, of grammar, of literary sources or by any other factor that influences the process. And ultimately communication is itself a process of bringing one part of the body, the hand or mouth, into relation to other bodies, and of expressing a figment of the imagination – the 'mind' – through all the available material instruments the body can muster.

Faces

One of the principal places where minds and bodies converge is the face. When *Titus Andronicus* has both Marcus and Titus try to 'read' Lavinia, it's her face they dwell on first, although gesture, posture and eventually writing all come into play as well. 'Thy cheeks look red as Titan's face / Blushing to be encountered with a cloud' (2.3.31–2) says Marcus, comparing Lavinia's human face in a most intriguing formulation: not only does Marcus cross boundaries of human and inhuman (Lavinia's human face is like the sun-god's, which – depending on how one chooses to see the reference – belongs either to a natural or a supernatural entity, personified and thus in possession of a face itself), he verbally marks (by observing out loud) the mark (the blush) that he compares to the sun's *hidden* shame (the sun's blush would be obscured by the cloud that causes it shame, rather as Lavinia might wish Marcus would stop remarking on her own face's betrayal of her violation and leave her in obscurity). The elements that make up this fleeting moment are complex: first, the idea that the body and mind are expressed through the face when the external blush signifies internal shame (albeit not very reliably, as we shall see); next the idea the blush exposes what the blusher wishes hidden, or 'speaks' in place of, and without the agency of the willed voice; and finally, what might seem like the most obvious and trite thing to point out, the idea that non-human things like the sun can be said to have faces and are therefore somehow like humans, capable of being personified.

The fact that faces are supposed to bring together minds and bodies and offer an observer significant information about their bearers is a common theme in Shakespeare's plays. The essays in James Knapp's 2015 collection, *Shakespeare and the Power of the Face*, bear that out by tracking the many ways faces function, not least in the contradiction that they can both hide and display emotion or characterological qualities. As David Goldstein puts it, the face is a site of 'epistemological, ontological, and ethical crisis. Is the face a mask or a mirror, a screen or a window?' (2013: 75). And yet, as Knapp says, the fact that it was such a problem does not diminish, and probably instead generates Shakespeare's characters' endless desire to read faces (8), and accounts for the surge of interest in physiognomy that informs his plays. Sibylle Baumbach's 2008 *Shakespeare and the Art of Physiognomy* notes that physiognomic analysis extended to other bodily attributes like posture (43): not only, then, were minds not enclosed by skulls or divided from bodies, but, as we've been finding throughout this chapter, the very thing that supposedly made a human recognizable to others *as human*, the face, was indivisible from the totality of the body. A face might say one thing; but shoulders, gait, even the degree of a body's hirsuteness might qualify what it said. Gail Kern Paster's work on Holbein's painting *The Ambassadors* uses this connection between the humoral body and the 'mind's' expression in the face to read against the grain of previous critics, finding that it is difficult for us to interpret the painting because we now lack the vocabulary of humours and the crucial role of skin colour it drew on (2009: 49). So faces are readable, but only with the full repertoire of disciplines that contribute to knowledge of the early modern body and world.

Shakespeare's treatment of the enigma of the face clusters around a set of factors. First, as Duncan discovers, faces do not do the work they are supposed to – they can obscure as well as disclose thoughts, intentions or character. In many cases, that duplicity is connected to either the body's role via the blood that suffuses the skin in the blush; or to the arts that can transform a face into a mask. In the first instance, characters like Hero in *Much Ado About Nothing* become the catalysts for an interrogation of how blushes are fundamentally equivocal. When Claudio rejects her at their wedding because he believes she has been unchaste, her father, Claudio and the friar argue over the 'story that is printed in her blood' (4.1.122): for Leonato, her blush is the same sign of her guilt as it is for Claudio ('She knows the heat of a luxurious bed; / Her blush is guiltiness, not modesty'; 4.1.39–40), but for the friar the 'thousand blushing apparitions' in her face signify her innocence (4.1.159). In some instances, the problem is that a face doesn't or can't blush: in *3 Henry VI*, Oxford is astonished that Warwick can mention his king's loss of French lands without 'betraying' himself with a blush for his 'treason' (3.3.97), while the fact that Othello's skin does not allow him to blush becomes, as Steven Swarbrick argues, an important part of the play's discourse on race and animality (2016). Early moderns were convinced that one who could not blush was therefore bestial, without shame. Othello's black skin is thus a case of what Derrida calls limitrophy, the establishment of boundaries that delimit a category or group – in this case the racial boundary that divides the unblushing Moor from blushing white Venetian society. Yet as Swarbrick points out, the racial logic of the play is not so simple: because white skin blushes *reactively*, rather than responsively (that is, mechanically, not because of reason), it can also be associated with an animalistic lack of control over the body. To blush or not to blush: either can implicate the blusher in discourses that dehumanize and bestialize him or her.

Blushes, almost all early modern examples attest, should tell a viewer *something* – but as often as not, as Swarbrick's argument demonstrates, they are debatable or missing altogether.[13] Or they are manufactured through some other materials, like cosmetics, that camouflage the face. 'I have heard of your paintings too', says Hamlet to Ophelia, 'God hath given you one face, and you make yourselves another' (3.1.144–6). Even an unpainted face can be mask-like, incapable of blushing or other expression, its illegibility a sign of the bearer's imperviousness to human emotion: York in *3 Henry VI*, confronts Margaret's cruelty by describing her as an 'Amazonian trull' with a 'vizardlike face, unchanging', asserting that he would 'essay to make [her] blush' were she not shameless (1.4.114–18).

Second, Shakespeare's faces are genetically iterative, distributed, and not necessarily individuating. Fathers' features are mirrored in sons, and brothers and sisters' in siblings, in ways that can defeat the assumption that human beings can claim unique identities, or even, in some cases, human identity at all. Orlando's resemblance to his father confirms his claim of identity in *As You Like It* when Duke Senior agrees that he must be Rowland's son, 'as mine eye doth his effigies witness / Most truly limned and living in your face' (2.7.197–8). That a son might carry the 'effigy' or painted image (limned) yet living in his own face suggests both the blurring of life and death and the repetition of the same via heredity. In *The Winter's Tale*, Paulina calls the newborn Perdita 'a copy of the father – eye, nose, lip, / The trick of's frown, his forehead ... The pretty dimples of his chin and cheek' (3.2.100–2). In the child's face, she tells the assembled court, they can find 'the whole matter' of the father, 'though the print be little' (3.2.99), imploring them to read the fine print and exonerate Hermione. The most extreme example of genetic copying, of course, is twinning, which features in more than one of the plays, but most fundamentally in *The Comedy of Errors*, which involves not one but two sets of twins mistaken for one another. Any certainty that identity inheres in, or is linked to, and therefore readable in facial features is completely undone by identical twins; correspondingly, the ability for one to claim one's home, one's business, even one's wife, or to be blamed only for one's own actions is disproven by the four main characters' experiences. Indeed, there is no such thing as the 'one' of the previous sentence, as the two Antipholuses and the two Dromios discover. Daisy Murray recounts the many and insistent ways that twins were considered monstrous by early moderns – evidence of maternal sin, defective, a kind of excess or surplus that violates the temperate mean (2017: 1–30, esp. 9–12). Science and religion agreed that twins were unnatural, uncanny. Of Viola and Sebastian, revealed together at the conclusion of *Twelfth Night*, Antonio exclaims: 'How have you made division of yourself? / An apple cleft in two is not more twin / Than these two creatures' (5.1.222–4). For a moment, Antonio reverts to the idea that a 'self' must be divided to result in two such identical faces; and he finds no better word than 'creature' to name both, a term that might imply a divide between human status and whatever these two are – that is, a term that registers the possibility that they are monstrous and imperfectly human.

What these examples illustrate is that faces can reflect lineage, an important function for early moderns concerned with securing things like inheritance through female chastity or the proper affiliations among noble families – but they do so at the cost of reliably performing another important work in conveying the specific individual thoughts and characters of their owners. They also suggest that 'ownership' of a face is a vexed subject. Further, they hint that reliance on the face as a – or in some instances, *the* – defining constituent of a universal-yet-individuated humanity may be based on flawed assumptions. In other words, we find in the complex representation of faces in Shakespeare's plays some resonances with recent debates in Western philosophy about the place and the function of faces, what Deleuze and Guattari call 'faciality'. In their analyses of the ethics of Shakespeare's use of the face, both Goldstein, on *Lear*, and Sean Lawrence discussing *Othello*, invoke the work of Emmanuel Levinas, whose premise that ethics is the basis of all philosophy is crystallized in the claim that encounters with the face of the other establish an obligation, whether (for Goldstein) to provide hospitality, in all its connotations, or (for Lawrence) forbidding murder (Goldstein 2015; Lawrence 2015). According to Levinas, the face-to-face encounter calls the subject into being, and takes the subject 'hostage', creating a responsibility to the other.[14] Levinas's conception of the face, however, has been thoroughly critiqued for its speciesist and humanist bias. Deleuze and Guattari, for instance, investigate the fact that 'faciality' is tied to a Western, European, white male face, the face of everything from images of Christ to Renaissance portraiture: 'The face is not a universal. It is not even that of the white man, It is White Man himself ... The face is Christ' (1987: 176). Derrida seizes on Levinas's equivocal answer to the question of whether animals have faces that issue the same call to responsibility: 'For declaring that he doesn't know where the right to be called "face" begins means confessing that one doesn't know at bottom what a face is, what the word means, what governs its usage, and that means confessing that one didn't say what responding means' (109). What a face is, Deleuze and Guattari suggest, is not a body part associated with the head, but a 'surface', a 'map' – it is 'the inhuman in human beings' (170, 171).[15]

While Derrida and Deleuze and Guattari deconstruct Levinasian faciality from the perspective of its exclusion of the animal and its limitation to 'the humanist schema of the visual and the scopic' (Wolfe 2010: 147), Katherine Behar mobilizes object-oriented feminism to question the anthropocentrism in what she calls 'vivophilia', or the privileging of lively, responsive dynamism in objects. Faces, Behar points out, are usually supposed to be alive, mobile, capable of creating meaning through expression (which relies on muscles, tendons, nerves all working actively together). A certain strategic necrophilia can interrupt this celebration of what is, like us, alive, and therefore agential. Correspondingly, Behar argues, materialists tend to resist self-implication in the networks of things they observe. For Behar, Botox is the answer. Botox quite literally introduces death into the lively visage of its user who injects a deadly toxin, but it also represents a 'necrophiliac form of plasticity', by paralyzing the muscles that make the face move and thereby preserving the face's aesthetic organization (2016: 135). A Botox-inhibited face loses muscle memory, and interrupts engagement with other faces, other humans, creating 'a new form of inner-directedness' (135) that constitutes the 'self' as an object.

In light of the various challenges posthumanist theory poses to the ontological and epistemological status of the face, we might therefore revisit the mechanism of some of Shakespeare's faces and perhaps draw some unexpected connections between disability and faciality. For instance, I see in Marcus's comparison of Lavinia's face to the sun's blushing visage a hint that faces do not, as Levinas might wish, restrict themselves to humans alone, that as Derrida and Deleuze and Guattari might argue, non-human objects often do have 'faces' that implicate them in the production of intersubjectivity. Let's recall that the last component of Marcus's description involves the personification of the sun as Titan, a poetic commonplace that perhaps goes unremarked *because* it is so common. The ability to find a face in the sun – or the moon, or a landscape, or any other object or set of objects – is an imaginative given. Yet it arises out of a fascinating and complex intersection of brain physiology and evolutionary adaptation; it is further a visual trait that organizes random information into reflections of the self-other divide.

Pareidolia, the process by which we discover faces in non-human objects, fascinated Renaissance artists of all kinds. For postmoderns, pareidolia often involves the organization of data with technological tools (that is, crunching large amounts of data via computer programs to reveal trends or problems whether in industry, government or business).[16] For early modern artists and writers, on the other hand, pareidolia usually involved faces, or other recognizable shapes, perceived in natural phenomena. Shakespeare's Hamlet, for instance, confirms his madness by engaging Polonius in a conversation about the shapes he finds in clouds:

> HAMLET
> Do you see yonder cloud that's almost in the shape of a camel?
> POLONIUS
> By th'Mass and 'tis, like a camel indeed.
> HAMLET
> Methinks it is a weasel.
> POLONIUS
> It is backed like a weasel.
> HAMLET
> Or a whale.
> POLONIUS
> Very like a whale.
>
> (3.3.367–73)

Given that Polonius's efforts at placating the 'mad' Hamlet immediately follows Hamlet's arrangement with a troupe of visiting actors to perform 'The Murder of Gonzago', the play in which he plans to 'catch the conscience of the king', we must consider how this playful recognition of animals in a cloud involves the same willingness to be tricked, even the pleasure involved in being deceived, that makes theatre and successful performance possible.

Unsurprisingly, artists were also thoroughly intrigued by pareidolia, and used it often. Albrecht Dürer's *View of the Val D'Arco* (1495) contains a hidden face that has been the subject of some dispute among art historians (not everyone thinks it's intentional, reminding us that we might be experiencing pareidolia ourselves, and can't distinguish that fact from any originary intention of the painter). Andrea Mantegna's *St. Sebastian* (*c.* 1480) more clearly uses a group of clouds in the upper left of the painting much as Hamlet does in Shakespeare: they clearly form a horse and rider. Indeed, Mantegna seems to have been particularly fond of using clouds to this end – his 1502 *Minerva Expelling the Vices from the Garden of Virtue* also includes a cloud with a face. Da Vinci, Giotto, Holbein and others all included hidden faces in non-human objects and phenomena. Da Vinci goes so far as to advise indulging in pareidolia as one means by which budding artists can develop the imagination:

> When you look at a wall spotted with stains, or with a mixture of stones, if you have to devise a scene, you may discover a resemblance to various landscapes, beautified with mountains, rivers, rocks and trees, plains, wide valleys and hills, in varied arrangement; often you may see battles and figures in action, or strange faces and costumes, and an endless variety of objects, which you could reduce to complete and well-drawn forms. And these appear on such walls confusedly, like the sound of bells in whose jangle you may find any name or word you choose to imagine. (1957: 37)

And as we will see in Chapter 5, Giuseppe Arcimboldo's composite faces made out of fruits and vegetables may owe their inception to the desire to capitalize on the same tendency of viewers to 'see' faces where none exist.[17]

Pareidolia has been the subject of a range of scientific studies, most of which have merely established that it is what is called a 'top-down modulated' response in the prefrontal cortex – a technical way of saying that actual visual perception, introduced to the brain via the visual cortex, is influenced strongly by other factors like mood, experience and expectation.[18] The prefrontal cortex is the site of executive function, planning, psychology, personality and other higher functions, so its role in arranging and managing information is what's important to the transaction. Pareidolia is a subset of apophenia, the tendency of the brain to organize random information into meaningful patterns; while pareidolia is usually assumed to be benign, apophenia is more often associated with pathology, either with conspiracy theories or, where it applies to the 'discovery' of voices in random noise, with misguided beliefs about the supernatural or life after death. Pareidolia and apophenia have been linked in recent popular culture specifically with the postmodern condition and with the information age, most saliently in William Gibson's 2003 novel *Pattern Recognition*. Gibson's protagonist, Cayce Pollard, experiences intense apophenia, which is both the source of her work as a trend spotter, and of her severe 'allergic' responses to branding of all kinds. She is 'a sensitive of some kind, a dowser in the world of global marketing', who has a 'violent reactivity to the semiotics of the marketplace' (2, 17). Pollard is drawn into a quest to reconstruct and find the source of random segments of video footage released onto the web – and indeed, the novel links identity with both the mass market and consumer culture that spins Pollard into nausea, but also with conspiracy theories, various kinds of underworlds and their forms of affiliation, and myriad forms of pattern-seeking. Her mother, for instance, is a believer in 'Electronic Voice Phenomena', and her father possibly involved in 9/11. Hayles, discussing Gibson's earlier work, observes that in contemporary literature, presence and absence is replaced by pattern and randomness, challenging physicality: 'Pattern tends to overwhelm presence' (1999: 35) something realized in Gibson's 'cyberspace', which makes data into a landscape without a physical referent. The posthuman emerges when 'computation rather than possessive individualism is taken as the basis of being' (Hayles 1999: 34). But at *Pattern Recognition*'s conclusion, when she encounters the footage's maker, Cayce is miraculously healed of her apophenic pathology – Gibson's lingering transcendentalism posits the dislocations of the present as disease, and a disease with a cure.

Could pareidolia also function as just such a disease? Is it in some way like Pollard's pathological allergy, a misfiring of the brain brought on by the translation of the environment into random deracinated patterns? Is it pathological, a 'disability'? If so, it is one that is common to all humans, one that might even define aspects of human cognition. One of the more interesting results of recent work on human vs. animal brain function has to do with how species-specific pareidolia is:

although there is increasing evidence that other species may have similar responses to visual stimuli (particularly having to do with anti-predator eyespots in animal colouration), science has as yet found no evidence that non-human animals have a penchant for ordering natural phenomena in precisely the way pareidolia or apophenia do.[19] Of course, for Renaissance artists and writers, there was no question that pareidolia was essentially human. Da Vinci's advice to seek patterns on stained walls to stimulate the imagination implicitly assumes that the capacity to find landscapes, battles, faces or costumes where none exist is a defining human talent, a peculiarity of human minds that elevates them because it makes possible the artistic creation of other unreal objects, worlds and landscapes.

Yet pareidolia sets up a problem in that it locks humans into a system that guarantees they see themselves in all things, whether human or not. That is, pareidolia is a kind of induced anthropocentric blindness to things as they are, rather than things as we perceive them. Rocks, clouds, landscapes, the sun, electrical outlets, burnt toast all become merely projections of ourselves. The dis/ability that has us face-hunting and face-reading, turning all things into us, requires a little of what Behar advises, a strategic denial of the face and a little temporary blockage of the 'other-directedness of the informatic self that is in connection' (136).

What might all this have to do with Shakespeare's plays? In its lovers' obsessive focus on facial beauty, *Love's Labour's Lost* offers an opportunity to think about the inhumanity of the face, its iterability, and the disability it incurs in those who dwell on it. The play is a rich source for the issues we've been discussing: it involves a failure of hospitality, masking, love of beauty, philosophical ambitions defeated by self-centredness, and above all, it keeps harping on faces. Indeed, it is possible to summarize the play as staging the power of pretty faces to disrupt humanism itself: H. R. Woudhuysen's introduction to the Arden edition calls the King of Navarre a 'would-be humanist monarch' (7) and Navarre's programme of withdrawal from the *vita activa* to study philosophy clearly establishes the play as a satire on humanist education. 'What is the end of study' asks the sceptical Berowne, facing down the king's desire to establish 'a little academe' (1.1.55, 13). Instead, the men are schooled by the Princess of France and her ladies, who confuse and control them during their quasi-military campaign of love. Hearing that the men are disguised as Russians, the Princess commands 'Ladies, we will every one be masked, / And not a man of them shall have the grace, / Despite of suit, to see a lady's face' (5.2.127–9) so that they might be mocked 'Upon the next occasion that we meet / With visages displayed to talk and greet' (5.2.143–4).

Masking, disguise and identity confusion are not unusual in Shakespeare's plays: from *Romeo and Juliet* to *Much Ado About Nothing*, *Twelfth Night* and *As You Like It*, they feature self-reflexive gestures toward theatre's fundamental investment in obscuring the body beneath the costume. But *Love's Labour's Lost* comes closer than most to dehumanizing the face in the process. Berowne defends Rosaline's beauty from the King's charge that she 'is black as ebony' (4.3.243):

> Is ebony like her? O word divine!
> A wife of such wood were felicity.
> No face is fair that is not full so black.
> KING
> O paradox! Black is the badge of hell,
> The hue of dungeons and the school of night
>
> (4.3.244–51)

Through a series of class- and race-based attacks on blackness, Berowne promises to 'prove her fair' until Longaville points to his shoe, saying 'Look, there's thy love, my foot and her face see' (4.3.270, 273). On the one hand this moment can be read for its convergence of xenophobia, the racializing of barbarism (Berowne calls himself 'a rude and savage man of Ind' and the King joins in mocking Berowne's elevation of blackness by invoking Ethiops; 4.3.218, 264), and sexuality (shoes can indicate baseness, and therefore sexual debasement). But reading it simply for its conflation of the human face with an object like a shoe makes some sense as well, since later in the play Berowne will again be the catalyst for a scene in which faces and objects collide. At the show of the Worthies, he joins in needling Holofernes:

> HOLOFERNES
> I will not be put out of countenance.
> BEROWNE
> Because thou hast no face.
> HOLOFERNES
> What is this?
> BOYET
> A cittern-head.
> DUMAINE
> The head of a bodkin.
> BEROWNE
> A death's face in a ring.
> LONGAVILLE
> The face of an old Roman coin, scarce seen.
> BOYET
> The pommel of Caesar's falchion.
> DUMAINE
> The carved bone-face on a flask.
> BEROWNE
> Saint George's half-cheek in a brooch.
> DUMAINE
> Ay, and in a brooch of lead.
> BEROWNE
> Ay, and worn in the cap of a tooth-drawer. And now forward, for we have put thee in countenance.
> HOLOFERNES
> You have put me out of countenance.
> BEROWNE
> False! We have given thee faces.
>
> (5.2.601–16)

In this cascade of objects that can stand in for faces, or have faces on them, or in some way present a face to the world, the whole idea of what a face is, what it means to have one, is thoroughly deconstructed, leaving Holofernes not merely disconcerted (put out of countenance) but denied a face altogether. In Levinasian terms, this might mean that the company of nobles has become inhospitable to Holofernes, denied his humanity. But the humanism of that reading is itself undercut by the sheer fact that everything under the sun – and, as Marcus makes clear in *Titus Andronicus*, the sun itself – has a face, thus disallowing the specific claim a human face might want to assert. There is no place for Holofernes to interpose his own face as distinct; he drowns in the flood of gifts from his noble audience. His face, like Rosaline's black face that can be compared to a shoe, is made an object among other objects, revealed as inhuman.

'This is not generous, not gentle, not humble', Holofernes laments (5.2.623). Indeed it isn't. But the corrective to his humiliation does not rest in the re-establishment of his human face. Rather, the noble men must be likewise outfaced by the intrusion of death, apparently the only thing that can drive them inward to discover their own situated knowledge of the world, and humble them with its anti-communitarian effects. At the news that her father has died, merriment turns to grief in the unexpected about-face of the play's final scene, and the Princess appoints to the men one year of study, this time in an 'insociable' environment where they may more carefully evaluate their attachment to the women (5.4.793). With no one to witness, no humanist subjects to study, the men accept a banishment that may educate them, like the hermits they must emulate, in the 'strategic misanthropy' Stephan Herbrechter suggests is worth adopting 'out of care for the human and a future of and for the human, including his or her natural and cultural environment' (2012: 55). At a minimum, their new 'academy' will redress their disability, their assumption that their countenances are what count. Like Behar's counterbalancing Botox-induced necrophilic paralysis, the men's fate temporarily interrupts the usual celebration of love-as-future-life (through marriage and reproduction), and resists the traditional humanist sentiments of comedic closure.

4

Neither Fish nor Fowl

In her influential meditation on the relationships between humans and companion animals, *When Species Meet*, Donna Haraway adapts Bruno Latour's insight that 'we have never been modern', observing instead that 'we have never been human'. By investigating the encounter between non-human animals and those human animals who work with them, cohabit with them, or just enjoy their company, Haraway challenges the boundaries of the category of 'the human': 'Once again we are in a knot of species coshaping one another in layers of reciprocating complexity all the way down. Response and respect are possible only in those knots, with actual animals and people looking back at each other, sticky with all their muddled histories' (2008: 42). When the fundamental exceptionalist distinction between species goes, along with it goes the division Latour also questions between nature (all that is non-human) and culture (all that is human-created) that seems to define modernity. Modern discourse, Latour points out, manufactures both disciplinary and related classificatory boundaries that it then works to keep pure, boundaries between, for instance, science, politics and religion along with their respective 'proper' methods or objects of study. Nature, the domain of 'the animal', is by this process separated from and distanced from 'culture', the domain of 'the human'. But as Haraway and Latour both argue, modernity also hybridizes, since whatever elements have been exiled in the name of purification sneak back into those supposedly discrete classifications. The result is an ongoing process of mutual contamination, of exchange, and lived interpenetration that resists the ordering impulses of philosophical and theoretical discourses. 'Naturecultures', ontological confusions that problematize traditional binaries, are thus a consistent focus of Haraway's work through both her two manifestos (1991, 2003) and related texts: hers is a de-anthropocentrizing anthropology that interrogates the philosophical assumptions about animals and animality that have attended, and, she argues, impoverished both philosophy and the world it attempts to describe.

Haraway is one of a generation of posthumanist theorists who analyse interspecies interactions as a principal part of a posthumanist agenda.[1] The study of animals has been integral in the development of posthumanism, in some ways even fundamental to it. Animals and the human/animal divide have motivated much of the politics impelling posthumanist writing and continue to motivate scholars and philosophers alike. The abyss that has historically separated human from animal has justified the material and ideological exploitation of the latter in the interests of the preservation of the former. Those concerned with the consequences of that distinction, and with making practical changes in policy and behaviour through a new ethics, politics, and metaphysics, have shaped broader debates in posthumanist theory. The metaphysical questions raised by the relative positioning of human vs. animal have been no less important. In the study of Shakespeare and early modern literature, these pressures have been productive. Building on an early body of what Erica Fudge has called 'hobby histories' involving animals, scholars in the period have found a cornucopia of beasts, analogical systems comparing humans with their non-human counterparts, debates about the nature of nature, and consideration of the ethical obligations humans owe those with whom they share creation (Fudge 2002). Nineteenth-century catalogues of, for example, the birds of Shakespeare gave way in the early and mid-twentieth century to historical or literary investigations of Shakespeare's uses for the menagerie that populates his plays and poems. Keith Thomas's *Man and the Natural World* (1983), provided a launching point for sustained and serious scholarly investigation. But in recent decades, an outpouring of scholarship on the animal-human divide has significantly complicated the picture of how Shakespeare's animals trouble or qualify definitions and concepts of 'the human'. Laurie Shannon has most trenchantly observed, for instance, that the playwright almost never uses the term 'animal', and when he does, he applies the word to human character or action (Shannon 2009). This indicates that the gulf we assume alienates humans from animals, one manifestation of the nature-culture divide, is historically specific and post-dates Shakespeare's moment. Indeed, the usual argument is that Descartes and the Enlightenment philosophy that followed his method, attempted to stabilize the absolute division of humans from animals based on animals' lack of reason. Prior to Descartes, the status of humans vs. animals was vexed; after Descartes, animals were 'beast-machines', inherently incapable of reason (Fudge 2006; Shannon 2013).

Whether this is an accurate or fully explanatory history in its specifics might be moot, but certainly early moderns, while they may have believed that humans occupied a different status from animals because they possessed a particular kind of soul, distinct from that with which (most) animals were endowed, were less secure that the distinction was clear, persistent, or a given for all.[2] Fudge argues that reason was a slippery quality, not always found in all human beings (2006), and Shannon elsewhere charts the ways animals seemed to possess either nature's greater indulgence and favour – in examples of negative exceptionalism that credited animals with better skills and inherent capacities than humans – or a right to a degree of justice, given their suffering for human sin (2013). Andreas Höfele has addressed the link between spectacles of punishment, the theatre, and the treatment of animals, finding that characters like Coriolanus or Falstaff most resemble baited bears (2011), making them victims whose subjection to brutal treatment satisfies society's and the state's need to establish distinctions. Bruce Boehrer has argued that the human-animal boundary was complexly porous, so that plays like *Midsummer Night's Dream* and *Merchant of Venice* stage the problematic bestialization of humans – the women of Athens, Shylock – while human character was established primarily through animal comparison in a reciprocal process that also changed how animals were viewed and treated (2002, 2010). My own writing has addressed the issue of animal embodiment, which deconstructs the material distinctions between humans and animals (2013a). Increasingly those working on early modern animals have embraced versions of posthumanist theory to illuminate early modern culture, and have proposed that works like Shakespeare's might provide a salutary counterbalance by reaching back to a moment that predates the Enlightenment philosophy undergirding some posthumanist theory.[3]

Perhaps the most influential animal-oriented philosophical meditation has come from Jacques Derrida, whose *The Animal That Therefore I Am* appeared in French in 2006, and in English in 2008. Practicing what he calls 'limitrophy', Derrida examines the borderline between human and animal that establishes the limits of both – what creates that limit, what sustains it and what might threaten or complicate it. In his engagements with Descartes, Heidegger, Lacan and Levinas, among a host of others, Derrida exposes the persistent, sometimes wilful, philosophical blindness regarding the animal that allows its relegation to *zoe*, mere finite existence or 'natural' life, and its exclusion from *bios*, or the 'good' life that has political and ethical relevance. Indeed, the idea of 'the animal' is itself an erasure of particularity that Derrida wants to resist; he coins the term '*l'animot*' (which plays on *mot*, French for word, yet sounds the same as the plural French *animaux)* to reflect language's role in oversimplifying and generalizing: 'Neither a species nor a gender nor an individual', he says, '[the *animot*] is an irreducible living multiplicity of mortals, and rather than a double clone or a portmanteau word, a sort of monstrous hybrid, a chimera' (2008: 41). Derrida insists on philosophy's – and human as well as 'human' – indebtedness to the animal other, and so interrogates the many ways that metaphysics has failed to acknowledge and remedy the anthropocentrism at its heart. The point for Derrida is not to eliminate difference, or erase the distinction of human from animal (for instance, by arguing simply that both are biologically comparable), but to multiply differences so that binaries become impossible.

Other theorists have taken up the challenge to rethink the status of 'the animal' from diverse perspectives, and, according to some critics, with varyingly useful results. In *A Thousand Plateaus*, Gilles Deleuze and Felix Guattari argue for the 'molecular' process of 'becoming animal', which involves the contagion of multiplicity, the lateral, unpredictable, unintended intermingling of non-static beings (1987: 232–309). Becoming animal has nothing to do with history, with imitation, or with imagination – any of these would simply re-impose the hierarchical thinking that underwrites most concepts of identity, will and reality. Instead, becoming animal involves being drawn into a zone where human and animal share affect, participate in an assemblage and establish a new relationship to the world. Haraway, who also finds Derrida's engagement with actual animals lacking, is sceptical about Deleuze and Guattari's preference for 'demonic' (and therefore disruptive) over domesticated (compliant) animals. Responding to their revulsion for 'little house dogs' owned by elderly women – their example of the epitome of the sentimentalized animal – Haraway remarks 'I am not sure I can find in philosophy a clearer display of misogyny, fear of aging, incuriosity about animals, and horror at the ordinariness of flesh' (2008: 30).[4] She finds the theory of Deleuze and Guattari a 'fantasy' that has little to do with actual animals and how they behave, how they organize themselves, or what humans and animals might actually do with one another. And yet, whether a fantasy like the abyss that has been fashioned between humans and animals can be countered effectively with another fantasy is a legitimate question. Others have noted that Deleuze and Guattari's various 'becomings' seem to occur strictly in the interests of a human subject. Yet certainly *A Thousand Plateaus* continues to motivate posthumanist study, even feminist versions of it, involving the human-animal relationship through its description of a fragile, always interconnected ontology.

Giorgio Agamben, another important voice among posthuman theorists and philosophers concerned with animals, has argued that biopolitics predates modernity, that it is in constructing differences between the human and the inhuman that sovereign power establishes and perpetuates itself (2004: esp. 13–16, 23–6, 33–8). Agamben maintains that the 'anthropological machine' by which the human being is generated out of difference from 'the animal' – from animal lives and from bare life as lived by something named the animal – is thus only rejiggered from time to time, to fine-tune it in light of current paradigms of thought. The 'state of nature' that repeatedly figures in philosophy (and political theory and economic thought) and is associated with animality is, Agamben makes clear, not something that precedes culture, but is produced by it: 'The state of nature to which civilized human man might "return" is not a state that he ever left. Rather it is an idea produced in and by the civilized order it is deemed to precede' (2004: 43). Agamben, like Derrida or Deleuze and Guattari, has raised as many questions as he has answered. For Matthew Calarco, for instance, the problem of what ethics is made possible by Agamben's work remains unresolved (2008: 79–102), and other writers note that Agamben's philosophical approach may provide little room for a consideration of 'actual animals', as Haraway might say, or for a way out of the exploitative structures that his analysis reveals.

What strikes me about these theoretical models is their convergences, rather than their different premises or possible limitations. The effect of posthumanist theory's engagement with 'the animal' or with animals has been to reorient our attention to, and trouble our assumptions about, what matters in a given text. Around the edges and within itself, the human subject frays, blurs, and recognizes itself as something other, as multiple: that is, to return to the word that I introduced at the beginning of this chapter, the human subject emerges as *hybrid*. In Derrida's and Deleuze and Guattari's work we have manifestations of something we might call human-animal hybridity, most broadly understood: either, as in Derrida's case, 'the human' and 'the animal' are the same-with-a-difference as well as the-same-but-built-upon-difference – *Ecce Animot*, writes Derrida (2008: 48) – or, as in Deleuze and Guattari's case, the animal other is capable of deconstructing the unitary, Oedipal version of the subject through contamination and 'becoming'. Hybrids are also essential to Agamben's machine, if not always highlighted by that name: the more violently the boundary between human and animal is enforced, the less clear it is, and the more confusing the status of the subject becomes. Ontologically, there is no such thing as a 'human being': manufacturing the human is an endless process of making something out of nothing, of defining 'human' by what it is not. And that process relies on the constant oscillation between whatever 'we' humans are, and whatever we imagine 'animals' to be. But for Agamben the modern, post-Enlightenment version of the machine has made this process internal – to be human requires containing or expunging the beast within (37) as well as dehumanizing certain external groups. Is this not a recipe that reflects a recalcitrant universal hybridity?[5]

I realize that the term hybrid used this way could become so unstably vague or general as to be less powerful, but it also might well be the best way to understand the desires that ground animal-oriented posthumanist theory. It is not that posthumanism asks us to simply imagine ourselves as non-human or animal; rather, it requires that we reject any version of the imagining ego or the material body that 'houses' it that is singular, monumental and fixed. Instead, we are invited to embrace vulnerability, uncertainty, comingling and rhizomatic excursions into otherness. Further, even the etymological origins of 'hybrid' and the term's botanical and mammalian expressions seem useful to our purpose here. From the Latin *hibrida* or *ibrida*, the word originally designated the offspring of a union between a wild boar and a domesticated pig; over time, the meaning shifted to designate the human product of a liaison between different races, a half-breed. The historical examples the *OED* gives for these two meanings show a gradual migration of the term, from the early 1600s when it was largely about boars and pigs, to a period when its meanings regarding mammals and humans overlapped in roughly the mid-seventeenth century, and then to later applications mainly to human, animal or plant offspring. Eventually, by the nineteenth century, the term also indicated any kind of mixture or heterogeneity, often with a disparaging inflection. The human denotation rests on a linguistic bedrock of animal reference, but grows away from, and in antipathy to, its animal origin, bleeding out into the world to encompass its flora and fauna. Posthumanism's invitation to hybridity undoes and reverses this migration, so that 'hybrid' is no longer a disparagement, and is also no longer only binary. The term might, as this chapter will demonstrate, also give us a new inroad into Shakespeare's plays, a path not always taken when seeking the animal, or animals, in them.

Hybridity has often been used in postcolonial theory to describe the consequence of colonial domination, which results in new catalyzed or creolized groups, individuals and practices. Cary Wolfe has remarked that it is the original distinction between human and animal that establishes the binary model through which all Others are created, a fact obscured in liberal rights discourse: in effect, the animal is the first subaltern, whose speech is unintelligible as language, and whose body is deemed suitable to be enslaved (2003: 7). The postcolonial hybrid is thus related to the posthuman in the sense that postcolonial mixtures might be said to be derived from the broader process by which 'the human' is first established as a thing that exists, and then given qualities like 'whiteness', 'civilization', 'masculinity', 'ablebodiedness' and so on. To achieve liberation from this state according to Enlightenment humanism, the human who is compared to a beast, whose animality is encoded as the source of her subjection, strives to root out and banish that which is 'bestial' in her thoughts or behaviour; she rejects her place among animals, aspiring to rise above them and join humanity, where rights and privileges are conferred. But this process will always remain incomplete, the resulting creature made not pure and whole, but confused and confusing. In short, she remains an irreducible (or untranslatable) hybrid.

If this latter description of the intersection of postcolonial and human-animal hybridity sounds familiar to Shakespeare's readers and audiences, it is because so many of his characters are hybrids that enact similar struggles. Caliban, named a fish-human hybrid, is offered education and admission to civilization by Prospero and Miranda; taught to speak, he finds, however, that his non-identity with the only 'true' humans on his island is merely accentuated, made more concrete. When he attempts to 'people this island' by raping Miranda, he is given a form of physical punishment and enslavement to match what Prospero judges to be his essential beastly nature. The result, as Caliban puts it, is that he has learned to speak only in order to curse (1.3.367); Prospero's constant torments have channelled and evacuated his acquisition of language, one of the defining characteristics assumed to constitute the human.[6] Caliban discovers that the promise of full enlistment in humanity was a fraud in part because 'humanity' requires others like himself against which it can be defined. If Caliban were to achieve full humanity, Prospero would, as Caliban puts it, have no 'subjects' (1.3.344), and so no sovereignty. Caliban aspires to create a race of his own (a 'people') on the presumption that he merits equality with other colonizers and nation-founders. But Prospero and Miranda refuse his enlistment in the ranks of humanity. He must remain 'villain', 'poisonous slave', 'hagseed', 'malice' and finally 'thing' (1.3.313, 322, 368, 370; 5.1.278).

While Caliban functions as the dark undertow to a romance narrative about loss and redemption, Bottom offers *A Midsummer Night's Dream*'s audiences a comic take on the same themes. The artisan performers, 'rude mechanicals' ('rude' indicates not merely stupidity but a lack of reasoning ability linked to animality, while 'mechanical' refers to a dimension of labour that is concerned exclusively with the material, rather than the abstract or theoretical), long to be 'made men' by success in entertaining Theseus and his noble peers. Bottom, the rudest and most irreducibly mechanical of the lot, is transformed by Oberon and Puck into an inverted centaur, with the head of an ass and the body of a human; Bruce Clarke points out that Bottom is not just a 'hybrid monster', the play's 'chief metamorph', but is hybrid in multiple registers – he embodies the human–animal distinction, but also crosses the human–fairy boundary, which no other character does (Clarke 2008: 77–8). At the play's conclusion, Bottom returns to human form, but then violates the formal containment of the play itself when he speaks across the boundary that should divide his impersonation of Pyramus from the audience that attends his performance. Titania, through the temporary effect of the love juice, falls in love with this hybrid and works hard at purifying him – but what Bottom has become after his metamorphosis is merely more himself, not fully human due to his lower-class status and his ignorance of the full content of the culture in which he tries to participate, but not wholly animal either. He neighs and longs for hay. Titania binds and silences him; yet even when 'liberated' from his bestialized condition, Bottom has no language, no speech with which to frame his experience. Instead, he borrows from and butchers 1 Corinthians:

> I have had a most rare vision. I have had a dream, past the wit of man to say what dream it was. Man is but an ass if he go about to expound this dream …. The eye of man hath not heard, the ear of man hath not seen, man's hand is not able to taste, his tongue to conceive, nor his heart to report, what my dream was.
>
> (4.1.203–9)

Language for Bottom, as for Caliban, is no more an instrument he can marshal successfully than it is the purview of a donkey or a goat. And yet, no audience in either Shakespeare's or our time would simply view Bottom as inhuman. For early moderns, the proposition that man is indeed but an ass is descriptive of whole groups among human beings – children, lower-class labourers, drunkards, the mentally disabled.[7]

Such obvious hybrids might lead us to imagine that Shakespeare finds hybridity only in select locations and situations, like the colonial world of Prospero's island or the magical landscape of Oberon and Titania's forest. Our review of some posthumanist animal theory, however, should make us aware that hybridity is the inevitable consequence of conceptualizing the world as if it were divided between two kinds of beings, human and animal.[8] When Shannon observes that Shakespeare uses the term 'animal' only eight times in his entire oeuvre, and in those cases he refers to human beings, not actual animals, she suggests that he does so because only a human can be animal in a world where animals are merely themselves.[9] Boehrer's accounts of familiar species – horses, parrots, turkeys, cats and sheep – as they are transformed and recast time and again according to changing social, religious and economic pressures reminds us of the metaphoric and material mutability of humans and animals. Erica Fudge meanwhile zeroes in on dogs, and finds that Lance's dog Crab in *Two Gentlemen of Verona* establishes the dividing line between civilized and uncivilized – and therefore is a primary instrument for constituting human identity (Fudge 2008). Indeed a substantial body of critical work in the period has evolved over the last two decades that deals with many specific kinds of creatures used in the plays to define aspects of human nature, or of human character. Even a cursory reading of Shakespeare turns up whole catalogues of non-human animals deployed metaphorically, metonymically or otherwise allusively to shape the audience's understanding of his fictional worlds and their inhabitants.[10] It is fair to say that as far as Shakespeare is concerned, it is impossible to know people without knowing them through or as animals.

A posthumanist analysis of Shakespeare's plays also holds, however, that no creature, including but not limited to Caliban or Bottom, can be made 'purely' one thing, and that no division between nature and culture is ever possible. Essentially, for a posthumanist reading hybridity is not a technique or a particular thing, but the ground on which 'the human' is constructed. All humans are products of mingling, of mixture, however they defend against that knowledge by attempting to offload the consequences of animality onto others. And so in the first portion of this chapter I take the opportunity to look for complex human-animal hybrids in unexpected places in Shakespeare's plays, indeed in every possible place, not only to emphasize that 'the human' is always already multiple and diverse, but also to suggest that 'humans' exist in an environment of shared being with the animals that populate history, myth and the material world around them. In fact, *A Midsummer Night's Dream* itself is populated by a number of less obvious hybrids than Bottom: audiences at the play would likely have remembered, for instance, that Theseus most famously killed the monstrous minotaur, a creature with the head of a bull and the body of a man, in the Cretan labyrinth; but the play also casts Lysander as a snake (in Hermia's suggestive dream of betrayal), Helena as a spaniel, and Hermia as a dwarf and a vixen. In this they are no different from the majority of characters in any of the plays who are constantly spoken of for their animal resemblances or animal qualities. While we might dismiss many such references as 'mere' metaphor, that would be a mistake – insofar as language constructs a version of identity, these metaphors and analogies fashion humans in terms of their animality to such a degree that it is difficult to distinguish one kind of being, human or animal, from another.

We might also consider that the practical, material circumstances that govern the English theatre ensured that any and every character might be said to be hybrid – a byproduct of the union of textual and spoken words, an actor's mammalian body and gestures, layers of clothing, the spatial influences of stage and theatre, and so on. Certainly the experience of watching a play in Shakespeare's Globe was likely to remind those present of their animality, not merely because this was a major thematic of many plays, but because the environment itself was full of animal sounds, smells and actions. The concept of 'apishness' was often used to describe foppish, foolish or antic human behaviour: Rosalind promises that as Ganymede she will be apish to Orlando in *As You Like It*: 'I will be more jealous of thee than a Barbary cock-pigeon over his hen, more clamorous than a parrot against rain, more new-fangled than an ape, more giddy in my desires than a monkey' (4.1.142–6). The Fool in *King Lear* sings of wise men turned apish in the topsy-turvy times Lear has ushered in:

> Fools had ne'er less grace in a year,
> For wise men are grown foppish;
> They know not how their wits to wear,
> Their manners are so apish.
>
> (1.4.158–61)

Nations and generations too could 'ape' those they admired, as York points out in *Richard II*: 'The open ear of youth doth always listen; / Report of fashions in proud Italy, / Whose manners still our tardy apish nation / Limps after in base imitation' (2.1.20–4). Holly Dugan traces the presence of baboons who were trained to perform on English stages, pointing out that their 'monstrous hybridity' was understood in terms of their 'bodily intimacy' with humans (2013: 84–5); that we are uncertain whether certain characters, like Bavian in *Two Noble Kinsmen*, were human or baboon suggests 'a stunning slippage between human and animal actors' (78). Actors on stage were always aping – sometimes aping their betters, sometimes simply aping foolish courtly manners or aping apes with their awkward capering – but the point of their acting might be to signal to audiences the degree to which those who were not by profession actors nonetheless performed like trained animals for their masters.[11]

How 'human' any given individual at the theatre or on stage could claim to be was under constant erasure by the very conditions of the location itself: for instance, the Globe was situated in the liberties of Bankside in close proximity to the bear garden with specific consequences for moments featuring animal allusions in the plays. Apes trained to perform in one location probably showed up in the other – monkeys that were used to ride dogs as part of the entertainment for bear-baiting audiences might show up in street performances or on theatrical stages as well. Dugan references the origin of the term 'jackanapes' in the tricks and japes of these creatures (2013). Caius in *The Merry Wives of Windsor* can't come up with a better derogatory term than ape for both Simple and Hugh Evans (1.4.101–3; 2.1), and Parolles gets the same treatment from Diana in *All's Well that Ends Well* (3.586). But bear-baiting contributed more to the plays, framing both comical and tragic forms of torture. Falstaff, while no jackanapes in *Merry Wives*, is positioned as a baited bear in his continued humiliations at the hands of Mistresses Page and Ford. Early in the play, Slender boast of having seen the famous bear Sackerson twelve times, which introduces the possibility that not only is Falstaff to be understood as a (human) poacher of women, but he stands in for the dangers of lustful, and therefore bestial, passions to Windsor's close-knit middle-class community. Bears were understood to be sexually rapacious as well as aggressive. Their position in the baiting arena, on hind legs (to free their paws for defence) fending off swift attacks from the dogs, might well have reminded baiting audiences along with playgoers that the upright posture of animals other than apes could equally echo human bipedalism. Certainly Coriolanus resembles nothing so much as a baited bear when forced to stand in the full view of the plebeians to show his wounds and respond to their questions (Höfele 2011: 92–114). These bestialized bear-men, however, were thought by some to simply mirror an audience's capacity to turn into brutes. Erica Fudge recounts the various voices censuring the sport of bear-baiting for its capacity to render 'humans' bestial in their blood-lust: faces distorted, voices incoherent, limbs akimbo, human audiences resembled the object of their attention. Fudge cites both Raphael Holinshed and Thomas Dekker, who find respectively monkey-baiting and bear-baiting discomfiting for the way in which these spectacles defeat the distinction usually drawn between human and animal, audience and performers: 'With their "shrill sounds and varietie of gesture" the humans themselves destroy the distinction between the watched animal and the watching human'. The very violence involved in bear-baiting, which is supposed to convey human superiority over wild nature, ends up destroying differences between species, between 'civilization' and barbarity, and between city and wilderness (Fudge 2000: 18–19).

Characters with no clear positional connection to apes, bears or other beasts are nevertheless tainted with the impurities of nature that bring them under the broad umbrella of the bestial. Jeanne Addison Roberts has offered an account of the 'hidden hybrids' in many plays, including in her analysis male-female hybridization (a desired thing in marriage), as well as figures like Amazons, masculine horsewomen who confuse multiple categories.[12] *Troilus and Cressida*'s Ajax is not merely one brute, but many rolled into one: Alexander describes him as 'valiant as the lion, churlish as the bear, slow as the elephant' (1.2.20–1), a veritable Noah's Ark of beastly qualities. Lecherous Saturninus in *Titus Andronicus* partakes through the various possible echoes of his name not merely of beastly passions and an astrologically based churlishness, but of the specific sexual excesses of the satyr, man-goat hybrid. Beatrice is a harpy in *Much Ado*, and Ariel received as one in *The Tempest*. Everywhere, entities are presented as composites, fusions of diverse types of both material and abstract being.

Hybridity, then, should be viewed not so much as the exception that delimits particular human identities, like those fashioned through the experience of colonialism, or even as an aspect of humans, but as the very baseline condition of human existence as early moderns perceived it. That prospect was especially evident for early modern playgoers, whose entertainments involved the consumption of many related kinds of spectacles in the arenas that shared real estate in Bankside. The workings of the 'anthropological machine' were often fairly unsubtle in Shakespeare's environment, not always well-cloaked but no less powerful as a result. And perhaps therefore they may be more easily recognized in posthumanist readings that attend to animals and animality. In what follows I offer an example of how refusing to limit the presence of hybridity to clearly embodied human-animal amalgamations like Caliban or Bottom can change how we understand the representation of human characters in at least one play in the canon. In a second portion, a brief coda that performs an ecomaterialist reading of Lance's speech in *Two Gentlemen of Verona*, I consider the space that is left *between* the 'neither ... nor' of this chapter's title, and find it a space not inhabited by binaries, as in the case of hybridity, but overpopulated by objects, among which the human is only an ellipsis.

My horse, my self

The most obvious and common hybrid human-animal in Shakespeare's world was the centaur. A creature of classical myth, the centaur migrated into multiple domains of early modern culture for its divergent significances. On the one hand, half-horse half-human centaurs were identified with brutal and indiscriminate animal passions: the most famous mythological tale involving centaurs concerns the rape of the Lapiths, a topic of plays, paintings, tapestries and poems throughout the period. Pirithous, King of the Lapiths, married Hippodamia, inviting the centaurs to the wedding; however, the centaurs became drunk and attempted to abduct the Lapith women and boys, prevented in a bloody battle by the Lapiths with the aid of Theseus, who was also a guest. *A Midsummer Night's Dream* glances at this tale when it features as the subject of one of the possible entertainments proposed for Theseus's marriage celebration. This classical source story has centaurs' human, rational capacity dominated by their bestial tendencies. Drink, as Cassio says, is 'an enemy in [men's] mouths to steal away their brains' (2.3.284–5), and leaves drinkers 'transform[ed] ... into beasts' (2.3.284–6). That the centaurs assault the Lapith women speaks to their bestial lust; but that they also attempt to kidnap young boys attests to their failure to make distinctions among 'natural' and 'unnatural' desire. When Iago tries to arouse Brabantio with the image of Othello 'tupping your white ewe' and 'making the beast with two backs' (1.1.87–8, 115) he not only highlights the presumption that Othello's blackness signifies his lecherousness, but proposes at the same time Desdemona's sexual indiscriminateness, and posits future offspring that, like the centaurs, will be animal-human hybrids. Lear's description of his unloving daughters, 'down from the waist they are Centaurs / though women all above' (4.6.124–5), shifts the gendering of the usually hyper-masculine centaur to convey Goneril and Regan's doubly unnatural behaviour. Eric Brown remarks that centaurs seem to have been for Shakespeare a bit of an '*idée fixe*'.[13] The figure of the centaur is one of the more obvious cogs in Agamben's anthropological machine. Mirroring in its physical hybridity both the external division of the world into human vs. non-human, as well as human interiority, supposedly comprising rational vs. beastly motivations and behaviours, the traditional image of the sexually indiscriminate, physiologically incontinent centaur does not so much bridge some imagined divide between nature and culture as produce the violence by which nature is banished from ethical, political inclusion.

However, this is not the whole story. The centaur was also an idealized point of comparison for horse–human interaction, as Philip Sidney – so aptly named 'phil-hippos', or horse-lover – makes clear in his *Defense of Poetry* and *The Countess of Pembroke's Arcadia*. In the former, Sidney ironically recounts the example of the great horsemaster Giovanni Pugliano, whose lauding of the animal, Sidney says, 'would have persuaded me to wish myself a horse'. If this backhand does not indicate a serious investment in horsemanship as the development of centaur-like ability, consider the *Arcadia*'s Mucedorus:

> But he, as if centaur-like he had been one piece with the horse, was no more moved than one is with the going of his own legs; and in effect so he did command him as his own limbs;

for though he had both spurs and wand they seemed rather marks of sovereignty than instruments of punishment, his hand and leg with most pleasing grace commanding without threatening, and rather remembering than chastising ... nor the horse did with any change complain of it; he ever going so just with the horse, either forthright or turning, that it seemed as he borrowed the horse's body, so he lent the horse his mind. (Sidney 1977: 248)

To display the noble qualities that make a horseman a fit ruler of men requires a union with the animal, a 'oneness' that challenges boundaries between human and animal. In Sidney's case, the assumption is that the human part controls the bestial – it is this that authorizes noble rule, guaranteeing that the bestial, whether within the individual or figured as the masses in relation, for instance, to a monarch, is under the rational management of the human part. Hence, early modern training of both horse and rider to the highest expression of skill was called the 'manege'. Shakespeare was well-acquainted with such a configuration of power and status: in poems and plays he repeatedly invokes the image of the centaur-horseman (see Watson 1983; Raber 1998; Flaherty 2011). But he does so to complicate its ability to confirm hierarchies of species or of blood. *A Lover's Complaint*, for instance, recognizes that an erasure of distinction might accompany the mutuality required in the centaur figure. The abandoned lover laments that her seducer was noted for his skill:

> Well could he ride, and often men would say,
> 'That horse his mettle from his rider takes.
> Proud of subjection, noble by the sway,
> What round, what bounds, what course, what stop he makes!'
> And controversy hence a question takes,
> Whether the horse by him became his deed,
> Or he his manage by th'well-doing steed.
>
> (106–12)

Although the language of sovereignty and subject, of nobility and command, are present here, so too is the threat that 'mettle' migrates from one body to another, and the education in the 'manege' might pass multidirectionally from horse to rider, or rider to horse. And centaur-riders do tend to love their horses too much. Hotspur in *1 Henry IV*, for instance, and the infantile Dauphin of *Henry V*, are paradigms of this confusion. Robert N. Watson and Boehrer agree that Hotspur's brand of centaur is doomed to fall to Prince Hal's superior self-mastery: Boehrer places him in the category that includes 'women, fools, and children' for expressing 'the bestial and childish impulses of a rebellious subject' rather than the Prince's cool, strategic rationality (Watson 1983; Boehrer 2002: 24). But Hal too is a horseman, simply one who rejects the animal centaur for celestial centaurism; he is described 'vault[ing] with such ease into his seat' on horseback, 'As if an angel dropped down from the clouds / To turn and wind a fiery Pegasus / And witch the world with noble horsemanship' (4.1.103–9).

Thus far we have been considering centaurs as if they all descended from the same source. In most instances, they were reputed to be the byproduct of a union between the Thessalonian King Ixion, and a cloud-goddess whose appearance is manipulated by Zeus to trick the lustful king who desired Zeus's wife, Hera.[14] As products of sexual desire crossed with trickery, their role as lawless beasts makes sense. But centaurs are more flexible, more labile than this single origin story would indicate. The lone centaur Chiron was supposed to be the child of an entirely different hybrid union, this between Kronos and Philyra, and as such offers an alternative and contrasting example of centaurine wisdom and restraint: unlike the excessive indulgence in drink and tendency to sexual predation of his brethren, Chiron enacts within himself the triumph of civilization over bestiality, which in Greek myth is what justifies his role as mentor to great heroes. This rational, noble centaur, however, seems to appear in Shakespeare's plays only once – in the apparently perverse naming of a character in *Titus Andronicus*, Tamora's son Chiron who, with his brother Demetrius, rapes and mutilates Lavinia.

Brown argues that centaurs are useful in part precisely because the same indeterminacy in the centaur's mythological history that allows the Lapiths' rapists and Chiron to coexist makes possible a greater degree of 'plasticity in metaphor', allowing Shakespeare to deploy paradoxical uses and meanings of the centaur image (1998, 177). That is how Brown explains Chiron's name in *Titus Andronicus*. But while Brown may be correct about the general flexibility of the centaur, given its divergent nature in myth, his claim that Shakespeare incorporates *both* origin stories is a bit misleading – there simply isn't a corresponding set of images or references that balances the Lapith-raping centaurs in the plays at all. Douglas Stewart has argued persuasively that the Chiron-as-educator narrative also informs Falstaff's role as substitute father-figure to Prince Hal in *1 Henry IV*, yet he carefully distinguishes the practice of *fostering* in the classical sources from Shakespeare's reliance on any direct representation of Falstaff *as a centaur*; indeed, if such a connection were to be made, one can only think that Falstaff's drinking and whoring would retroactively constitute Chiron as a charter member of the drunken Lapith-raping centaur clan (see Stewart 1977). So when we encounter the wrenching misapplication of Chiron's name to Lavinia's bestialized and bestializing rapist, the reference might merely seem to remind us that for Shakespeare the only good centaur is a remote and dead classical centaur whose name alone remains mobile for ironizing purposes.

This, however, is not a conclusion that fully accounts for the complex ways that Chiron figures in *Titus Andronicus*, nor for the network of mythological allusions within which the character is situated. Nor does such a reading explain how the mythological Chiron's alternative relationship to the natural world, both human and non-human, is put in play by his alter-ego's appearance in *Titus*. In fact, I think that rather than fulfilling his role as a figure for human control over, and useful exploitation of nature, and thus for a positive distinction between human and non-human, Shakespeare's Chiron momentarily jams the anthropological machine (to borrow Matthew Calarco's phrase; 2008: 79–102), derailing it by abyssally layering its referents, and thereby sabotaging its cultural work. In the remainder of this section, I consider the ways in which *Titus Andronicus* offers us a glancing but powerful case of the human-as-human/animal-hybrid, one that universalizes hybridity itself as a quintessential condition of being 'human'.

The mythic Chiron, unlike his bestial brothers, was immortal, quasi-divine[15]; he married, which ensures his association with the respect for law and custom that underwrites civilized behaviours. Himself the beneficiary of tutoring by the gods, he in turn passed his knowledge of medicine, hunting and music to human heroes like Achilles, Jason, Heracles, Aeneas and Odysseus, among others. Stewart points out that any centaur's wisdom derives from a close connection to nature – indeed, his very wildness leads to the 'wisdom of excess', and to a 'deeper than normal penetration into the nature of the world and the possibilities of life' (Stewart 1977: 7). Chiron was gifted with prophetic knowledge, a fact that allows him to be mobilized also in an early Christian tradition, as does his status as the first physician. Nature, in early Christian theology, organizes around two poles: on one side lies its hostility to human agency, coincident with the more common centaurs' rejection of marriage, and their violation of hospitality (as in the Lapiths' case), but on the other lies its supernatural, superhuman dimension, its function as a pathway to understanding God (Miller 1996). Chiron stands for the latter aspect of nature. Because he is a 'lone centaur', an individual with no peers, Chiron may also be the ancestor of the religious hermit, whose remoteness from human society and connection to nature gives him unique insight into divinity.

But Chiron in early modern texts can also appear as the avatar or the essence of the humanist scholar himself. Gary Schmidt points out that Chiron's role as instructor to great Greek heroes can be used to reflect the idealized role of the humanist councillor. Alciato's emblem 146, for instance, uses the image of Chiron to advise that 'whoever cares for kings should be a teacher who is half a beast, a centaur who is half a human' (2013: 47). Elsewhere, Thomas Becon describes the configuration of the schoolmaster's spiritual parentage as centaurine: Becon's *Catechism* credits the cultivator of mind for doing more than he who treats only the 'gross' body of a child to lift his student out of the level of brute beasts (cited in Schmidt 2013: 47). Indeed, Schmidt makes the case that figures like Elyot and Erasmus, by 'domesticating' classical learning necessarily had 'an ambiguous relationship with both the pagan past and the corrupt Italy' of the present age (the English held the work of early continental humanists, especially Italians, in suspicion for their Catholicism). Thus the humanist scholar straddled nations and time periods to achieve a centaur-like hybrid body of knowledge.

In knitting all these disparate representational qualities together, Chiron's name is essential: it translates literally from the Greek *kheiron*, or hand, and stands metaphorically or symbolically for human creative intervention in nature.[16] Chiron thus functions as the first, mythic, version of *homo faber*, defined by his ability to control the environment through tools. In any centaur's physical composition, it is those human hands as much as any facial features that distinguish him as hybrid. Hence, the emphasis on hands in many early centaur illustrations on Greek vases or in mosaics that have the centaur holding something, usually a bow and arrow or spear for hunting. Part of Chiron's appeal as an educator of heroes was thus his skill with the instruments of the hunt, combined with an intimate knowledge of animal behaviour. But it is his medical skill that connects him to a putative human capacity for godlike mastery over nature's production, with the implication that his intervention in his pupils' lives gives them therapeutic powers essential to an ethically just ruler. Chiron was associated with the linden, into which his horrified mother was transformed by Zeus (linden leaves, flowers and bark were used to treat fever, heart arrhythmia and other maladies), and with the more general use of herbs, drugs and spells in the treatment of disease. It was this knowledge he passed on to Asclepius, making Chiron, along with his pupil, a 'father' of medicine.[17]

Among all the parts of the body, the hand has special weight in early modern natural philosophy: God has endowed humans with 'Two wondrous weapons', explains Helkiah Crooke, 'which he hath denied to all other living creatures, Reason and the hand' (1615: 729). If bodily uprightness in humans supposedly renders them superior to animals by placing the organ of reason quite literally closer to God, it is also true that bodily uprightness frees the hands to bring human beings' godlike shaping power to their world. Hands are the direct physical channel through which reason influences the world; they even 'speak', as if they were a kind of tongue: John Bulwer's *Chirologia* (1644: preface), argues that gesture is as much a part of language as speech, 'for as the Tongue speaketh to the Eare, so Gesture speaketh to the Eye'. In fact, the hand acts as a second 'fountain of discourse', with detailed principles that can be recorded and understood by anyone, whatever their native tongue.

Katherine Rowe has argued that hands in Renaissance anatomies and other texts are vehicles of agency, complicated by the hand's simultaneous status as conveyor of interior will and its ability to grasp, wrest, assault or create beauty and reveal God's design in nature (1997). In the introduction to his *De Fabrica*, Vesalius advocates 'hands-on' medicine, combining all the various disciplines, not least surgery, which had been ceded to the 'barbers':

> It therefore follows that beginners in the art must be urged in every way to take no notice of the whisperings of the physicians ... but to use their hands as well in treating, as the Greeks did and as the essence of the art demands, lest they convert a crippled system of learning into a curse on the whole of human life. (Vesalius 1999: l)

Hands, therefore, become closely linked to the best practices of medicine in the Renaissance, illustrated by anatomists' inclusion of pointing, active, revealing hands in so many of their works. Bernard F. Scholtz finds that severed hands, arms and legs used in the emblem tradition signify disembodied will, ambiguously belonging to either God or to humans (Scholtz 1989).

There is a clear connection, then, between the centaur's possession of human hands and his access not just to medical knowledge – any animal might 'know' what plant to go to for respite from illness or discomfort – but to the ability to turn that knowledge into active healing, which confirms both Chiron's godlike origins, and his godlike superiority to any other centaur (and most humans). It is thus meant, I would imagine, to be scandalous that *Titus*'s Chiron not only perverts the anti-centauric 'civilized nature' announced in his name by raping Lavinia, but that he wrenches and distorts the image of the rational medical hand of exploration we find in anatomy texts by cutting off her hands along with her tongue.[18]

Chiron's actions are not merely an inversion of the centaur's meaning, however – that is, if the mythic Chiron is an anti-centaur, this one is not merely an anti-anti-centaur. He does not simply reinstate the rule of the bestial in the face of Rome's claims to civilization. Yes, he hunts and kills Titus's 'dear deer' (the 'dainty doe' (2.2.26) in Demetrius's words) with an 'unrecuring wound' (3.1.89–91); yes, as a warped 'educator' he carries out the lesson his mother prefers to those softer lessons Lavinia encourages when she remarks 'do not learn her wrath' (2.3.143). Chiron breaks down more than the human/animal distinction. Chiron's actions do not simply bestialize Lavinia; they return her to a *vegetative* state. Marcus laments her condition: 'What stern ungentle hands / Hath lopped and hewed and made thy body bare / Of her two branches'. Or perhaps she was a plant all along: 'Oh, had the monster seen those thy lily hands / Tremble like aspen leaves upon a lute'. In Marcus's response, she becomes landscape as well: 'Alas, a crimson river of warm blood / Like to a bubbling fountain stirred with wind, / Doth rise and fall between thy rosèd lips'. And her blushes are meteorological: 'Yet do thy cheeks look red as Titan's face / Blushing to be encountered with a cloud' (2.4.16–18; 44–5; 22–4). Most analyses of the play that focus on the animal/human boundary implicitly assume that all degradation of the human must end in the animal, but in Lavinia's case the regression seems endless, a more complete fall down the ladder of creation.[19] We might remember that in Titus's lament for his sons, he accepts Lucius's observation that he might as well 'recount [his] sorrows to a stone' (3.1.29):

> yet plead I must,
> And bootless unto them.
> Therefore I tell my sorrows to the stones,
> Who, though they cannot answer my distress,
> Yet in some sort they are better than the tribunes
> For that they will not intercept my tale.
> When I do weep, they humbly at my feet
> Receive my tears and seem to weep with me
> ...
> A stone is soft as wax, tribunes more hard than stone;
> A stone is silent and offendeth not,
> And tribunes with their tongues doom men to death.
>
> (3.1.34–47)

More than once, the play raises the possibility that rather than enforcing hierarchy, a chain of being with humans at its apex, nature retains no categories of meaningful difference and is perfectly capable of levelling all. Here Titus compares tribunes invidiously to stones, but lurking in his imagery, and in Lavinia's transformation into a plant or river or sun, is the suggestion that there is no way to produce comparison, analogy or systems of binaries that would distinguish among humans, plants, animals, weather or geological artefacts like stones.[20] Chiron, who is specifically *not* a centaur but 'simply' a human, already personifies this very possibility – and he imposes that knowledge on the Andronici through Lavinia's rape and mutilation.

Instead of plucking herbs from the field to cure Rome's ills as would his mythological antecedent, this Chiron 'prunes' Lavinia of the usual instruments of human agency by plucking out her tongue and hacking off her hands. Chiron has left her with no access to 'sweet water' to wash her wounds (2.4.6). We should think of Lavinia at this moment as emblematic of Rome's and the Andronici family's ability to reproduce something it believes is 'civilization', in contrast to the barbarous Goths. Chiron undoes that distinction. And again, it isn't just that Chiron is 'bestial' in what he does to Lavinia (which pretty much every one of the Andronici would happily call him), since by his name he already internally embodies a hybridity that encompasses the bestial, and because that binary is in fact *too stable* for what the play is suggesting. Rather, Chiron's wilful hand has exposed the failure of civilization *tout court*, its inability to arrive at a curative potion or herbal remedy, perchance plucked by a hybrid physician-centaur's hand from the bounty of nature, for a form of violence that is foundational, not incidental, to its existence.[21]

This may explain why the play's only other mention of centaurs confuses Chiron, who we have seen is usually considered the polar opposite of his wilder brethren, with the crowd of rampaging centaurs who violate the decorum and hospitality of Pirithous's wedding feast, and then further makes a mistake about whose feast that mythic tale involves. As he prepares to grind Chiron's and Demetrius's bones 'to powder small' to bake them in their 'coffins' (5.2.198, 188), Titus urges: 'Come, come, be everyone officious / To make this banquet, which I wish may prove / More stern and bloody than the Centaurs' feast' (5.2.201–3). At first glance, Titus's hands transform a human into meat, and in so doing confirm Chiron's innately violent, poisonous, uncivilized nature – he is not fully human, but centaur, a bestial man, and so is insufficiently different from the animals one hunts and kills for food. However, the slippage in Titus's formulation suggests something more. It was not, after all, *the 'centaurs' feast*' but the Lapiths' that was disrupted by the centaurs' assault on the Lapith women (and boys). The feast was intended to celebrate Pirithous's marriage to Hippodamia, literally 'the horse tamer'. Presumably Hippodamia tamed horses with bit and bridle – and hand.[22] In other words, the *feast of the Lapiths* was meant to celebrate a figure who represented the primacy of the human hand in controlling bestial nature – that is to celebrate exactly the model embodied by the mythic Chiron himself. By reassigning the feast to *the centaurs*, however, Titus removes any option that would affirm human agency over some externalized 'nature', figured in the horse/rider combination, or its horse/human analogue; he correspondingly also identifies himself with the centaurs, the provider of an already perverted, uncivil hospitality.

What's important, then, isn't that Chiron mirrors or embodies a hybridity that involves the division of the human from the animal or from nature, it's that Chiron erases even the possibility of a difference between human and animal, human and nature. That in turn makes the whole idea of a 'civilization' that can control, adapt, or instrumentalize nature laughably unattainable. There is no process by which the 'bestial' can be purged from the 'civilized' – such a formulation is rendered meaningless in Shakespeare's centaur references. Chiron exposes the 'bêtise' (to use Derrida's term for the foolishness involved in the idea of a 'singular' animal (2008: 18)) of thinking otherwise. Or perhaps to put it in more absolute terms, Chiron's name is no accident in that it speaks volumes about a difference that can make no difference at all, a proposed binary between 'the human' and animals, plants or other non-human entities, that undoes itself in the most violent fashion. The mythic Chiron promised dominion over nature to whatever constituted the 'human'. Shakespeare's Chiron denatures that myth, breaking down the distinctions that would make sense of such a promise.

In the middle: Animals as meat and leather

This chapter's title references a common saying, used to describe something that seems to have no category. It invokes a potential middle term – neither this nor that – by naming two things (fish, fowl) that occupy vastly different ranges of the environment, but it does so via a negative, 'neither'. In this manner, the title signals the absence, the aporia at the heart of all attempts to define or describe 'the human' that writers as different as Agamben, Haraway, Fudge or Wolfe have noted. My discussion of Chiron discusses human hybridity in terms of human intersectionality with another familiar, charismatic mammal, the horse. Unlike Caliban's hybrid nature as half-fish but half-man, centaurs at least share a geography and an elemental compatibility with human beings, which would have been accessible to Shakespeare's audiences. There are clearly just more horses 'on the ground' in early modern England than there are other sorts of animals – only the dog occupies a similarly ubiquitous place, and the dog's status is complicated by its ongoing reputation as vermin, prone to currishness. Many theatre-goers rode or cared for horses, saw them daily ridden and cared for by others, and/or were familiar with the artistic traditions that elevated the horse for its aristocratic and military associations. Centaurs may thus be more broadly imaginable and appealing, and so more common in the literature. In contrast, it is difficult to envision what a Caliban would look like at all, whether he would 'naturally' occupy only one realm (land or water), or whether he would cross those boundaries – certainly part of the point, since his appearance on stage highlights the imaginative representational dimension of theatrical spectacle. Brian Alkemeyer makes the case that rather than attributing human-like reason to apes, as one would now (and therefore finding apes potential exemplars of a kind of boundary-crossing), early moderns found the elephant the most rational of animals, most potentially like human beings (Alkemeyer, forthcoming). But who had seen an elephant – less available as spectacle than apes – in the flesh? Few or none of those attending the theatre in London, surely. Thus, based on what early moderns knew about animals, I have chosen the centaur as most effective in bearing the burden of my broader analysis of hybridity at work in fashioning a posthuman interrogation of species distinction in the plays.

What early moderns *did* know most thoroughly about mammalian animals 'in the flesh' had more to do with the practices of eating them and wearing them. When animals become clothing and food, they move across, confuse or confound different boundaries: of life vs. death, subject vs. object, inside/outside, active/passive and so on. Cartesian theories of 'the beast-machine' justify the use of animals in a more absolute fashion than even religious doctrine might have done for previous eras. The status of animals in relation to human sin and punishment, and the exact requirements for human 'dominion' over them are more complicated than a simple hierarchy might imply (see Shannon 2013: 29–81). Descartes 'solves' the problem of animal vs. human embodiment by asserting that both groups have bodies, but only human bodies house reason, and therefore have intention, agency and soul. Animals *are* their bodies for Descartes, mere objects put in motion by sense, an inferior motivating force (see Fudge 2006: 147–62 and Shannon 2013: 183–98). Yet for posthumanist theory, that object-status is not the clear and resounding 'truth' it was for Descartes. Ecomaterialists, for instance, would argue that in wearing and eating animals humans evidence their entanglement in their environments. Certainly the denouement of *Titus Andronicus*, which involves the translation of human flesh into meat pies, flattens otherwise important distinctions between species. While it is horrifying to the audience to recognize a taboo being violated, it is clear that Tamora and Saturninus have no clue that what they are eating is not animal in origin until they are told. All dead, cooked flesh looks, feels, and tastes pretty much the same.

As I note in the introduction, the new materialism's place in connection to posthumanist theory is well-established. Building on the methods and ideas of new materialists like Bruno Latour, Jane Bennett, Ian Bogost, Graham Harman and others, ecomaterialists (who employ the new materialisms with the goal of changing humans' relations with the environment) likewise treat the world of humans, animals, objects or phenomena, as flat, levelling them in the interests of refuting anthropocentric assumptions about hierarchies of value. Hence, what is seen as 'alive' is anthropocentrically assumed to be more important than what is 'dead' because *we* are alive and find that state of being a privileged form of existence. But, as ecomaterialists might point out, what we think of as 'dead' often is either composed of vital elements (think of soil, which is both mineral and decomposed vegetative matter, is the home of myriad tiny organisms, and which passes constantly through the guts of worms or other creatures including human beings), or has a kind of 'agential' function despite its inert condition – thus a piece of plastic, while not an agent in the traditional sense of intentional action, can, through its off-gassing, affect the cellular tissue of human lungs, causing discomfort or disease (Alaimo 2010).

Animal byproducts like meat and leather provide a specific set of examples of such agential complexity. Michel Serres examines the false distinctions that persist in our definition of ourselves as ontologically different from parasites; the sciences, especially, would like to deny that large animals and humans can ever be parasites – they must be hosts or predators because 'we do not live in the animals we eat' (Serres 2007: 9–10). But in fact we do, in their skins, feathers, in silks, so the bright line science draws between 'us' and 'them' is revealed to be merely a fable, a story we tell ourselves about who we are. Early moderns not only 'lived in' skin, feathers and silks, but 'lived off' of animals in ways that made human parasitism obvious. Thomas Browne observes in *Religio Medici* that the biblical reference telling us

> *all flesh is grass*, is not onely metaphorically, but literally, true; for all those creatures we behold are but the herbs of the field, digested into flesh in them, or more remotely carnified in our selves. Nay further, we are what we all abhor, *Anthropophagi* and Cannibals, devourers not onely of men, but of our selves; and that not in an allegory, but a positive truth: for all this mass of flesh which we behold, came in at our mouths. (Browne 1926: 60)

Humans digest the world; they survive only off the products of creation, including animals, but not limited to animal flesh alone, since all flesh has its origins in the assimilation of other forms of matter – the vegetables consumed by cattle, for instance, that were in turn fed by soil in which human corporeal remains (from composted shit to actual corpses) have decomposed. This 'circle of life' moment for Browne is meant to encourage Christian humility and therefore comfort its readers. What I want to highlight in Browne's formulation, however, is his reference to Anthropophagi and Cannibals, monstrous foreigners who are singled out in texts from Pliny to Shakespeare's *Othello* for their terrifying violation of 'natural' categorical distinctions, in this case between what is proper to eat and what is not.[23] But in an important sense all meat-eating is potentially an invitation that some other alien thing to take up residence within one (again, making each human not so much a hybrid as a collective): one's consumption of meat may lead to the ingestion of living creatures who feed off one's body, i.e. worms; or it might convey into one's gut materials not intended as food, like metals or poisons. The communal dimension of eating can also fulfil the literal meaning of parasitism, 'to eat beside'. David Goldstein argues that meals are occasions of 'opening' that 'interconnect our compartmentalized selves' with others at the table through everything from open mouths to open hearths and open dishes (2013: 4). In *The Merchant of Venice*, Shylock refuses Bassanio's offer of a shared meal not only because he will not eat pork, but because he rejects 'commensality' with Christians, Goldstein points out. Failed feasts in *Timon of Athens* and *Macbeth* are registers for audiences of eating's fragile role in establishing bonds, whether social or political. We are all parasites, I'm arguing, not only because we inhabit the skins of others, and are inhabited in turn by them, but because we invest such importance in *eating beside one another*.

If, however, humans are parasites, their elevation in the Great Chain of Being comes to look like a monumental fraud. What demotes humans from divinity and equality with the angels is embodiment, the requirement to eat flesh, which aligns in a postlapsarian world with human mortality. Fudge describes the basis of early modern resistance to vegetarianism as a religious issue: in avoiding meat, Christians would hubristically avoid acknowledgement of their fallen nature (Fudge 2004). Although, as Simon Estok has claimed, some of Shakespeare's plays seem to advocate a proto-vegetarian ethic, in general early moderns were not tolerant of the practice of eschewing meat (Estok 2007). Disciplining the body was all well and good, but in Protestant England, purification did not come through saintly sanctification, but through God's invisible and unknowable grace. Let's recall Latour's model of post-Enlightenment dehybridization, which involves purifying categories, but also bodies and minds. For early moderns, purification where food was concerned was held in great suspicion, and anyone who attempted it incurred serious moral and spiritual danger. Bodies were gross masses, in Browne's words, and humans were inevitably 'carnified'.

In the midst of every human, that is within the fleshly matter that made a human body, lay the stomach, receiving and digesting things other than itself, even providing a hospitable environment for certain creatures like worms. But every human also resided within external layers of animality, namely furs and leathers. In other words, from within and without, humans dwelled in the midst of non-human matter, a kind of ellipsis or conjoining grammar that held together inside and outside. As the son of a glover, Shakespeare would have been familiar with the processes by which animal skins became items of clothing and other useful objects. Traces of such objects' origins and composition often become conjugates in fashioning the plays' human characters. Erica Fudge concludes that King Lear is rendered, rather like a glove, an animal-made object through the course of Shakespeare's play (2012). Fudge finds in ecomaterialist theory a way to address the prevalence of animal byproducts in early modernity without entirely effacing the 'active presence' of animals. Human worlds are only 'so-called' in that they are created by multiple species; subject and object are always intimately connected, entangled in ways that defy the active/passive binary usually attributed to them. Fudge traces Lear's references to skins and perfumes, discovering that when he throws off his 'lendings' (3.4.106) it is because he has come to find skins and other coverings for the human body 'recalcitrant', defiant rather than passive possessions. His subsequent call for perfume – 'Give me an ounce of civet' (4.6.126) – is, in Fudge's analysis an attempt to reestablish human superiority and authority by having a more properly compliant object brought to him; but, ultimately defeated in that quest, Lear himself becomes a 'Renaissance animal thing' (2012: 56).

Fudge's reading of animal matter in *King Lear* is a brilliant example of what a posthumanist materialism can contribute to Renaissance animal studies, and vice versa. Shakespeare offers another, more comedic example of the entanglement of matter, human and animal, living and dead, one that involves leather's elevation and a human being's demotion among an assemblage of objects. Lance's harangue of his dog Crab in *Two Gentlemen of Verona*, upon his departure from court, might serve here as a parodic counterpoint to Lear's expulsion from his daughters' homes. Lance is heading to court with his master Proteus, but when he takes leave of his family, his dog fails to appropriately mourn his departure:

> I think Crab, my dog, be the sourest-natured dog that lives: my mother weeping, my father wailing, my sister crying, our maid howling, our cat wringing her hands, and all our house in a great perplexity, yet did not this cruel-hearted cur shed one tear: he is a stone, a very pebble stone, and has no more pity in him than a dog: a Jew would have wept to have seen our parting; why, my grandam, having no eyes, look you, wept herself blind at my parting. Nay, I'll show you the manner of it. This shoe is my father: no, this left shoe is my father: no, no, this left shoe is my mother: nay, that cannot be so neither: yes, it is so, it is so, it hath the worser sole. This shoe, with the hole in it, is my mother, and this my father; a vengeance on't! there 'tis: now, sit, this staff is my sister, for, look you, she is as white as a lily and as small

as a wand: this hat is Nan, our maid: I am the dog: no, the dog is himself, and I am the dog – Oh! the dog is me, and I am myself; ay, so, so. Now come I to my father; Father, your blessing: now should not the shoe speak a word for weeping: now should I kiss my father; well, he weeps on. Now come I to my mother: O, that she could speak now like a wood woman! Well, I kiss her; why, there 'tis; here's my mother's breath up and down. Now come I to my sister; mark the moan she makes. Now the dog all this while sheds not a tear nor speaks a word; but see how I lay the dust with my tears.

(2.3.5–31)

Both Fudge (2008) and Bruce Boehrer (2002) offer readings of this passage's treatment of Crab's role in determining what a 'human being' (i.e. Lance) is, but neither critic chases down the full context of the speech's muddling of shoes, dog, cat, human bodies, family members and other objects. Maids howl, and cats wring their hands – those defining appendages we saw mattered so much in our analysis of Chiron are here transferred to an animal outright. Shoes stand for parents based on their holiness (one has a 'worser soul' because it has a vaginal hole in it), staffs for sisters, hats for maids and dogs for people. What's more, dogs are expected to speak, to show emotion, much as the collection of animals and people mentioned all do. Crab of course violates this expectation; he is more inert than the objects Lance gathers to speak in place of his family here. Nor is the assemblage complete yet: when Panthino enters to warn Lance that his ship is sailing, Lance is called 'ass', and misunderstands 'tide' for 'tied', which he thinks refers to his tied dog Crab. The dialogue continues with a 'who's on first' routine that puts floods, tongues, tales and tails into spinning, echoic substitution. The linguistic pyrotechnics, however, extend rather than contrast with Lance's initial collection of people, animals and things, so that words join the assemblage as simply one more kind of object.

Do leather shoes resemble people in some fundamental way? As we saw in Chapter 2, according to Longaville in

Love's Labour's Lost shoes and faces can be considered at least fleetingly interchangeable; but is it merely foolish to ask a leather sole to also stand in for a man with a soul? Or one with a hole in it to represent a woman, defined by her genitalia? Or is there an allusion in this scene, with its myriad transferences between living and dead, animal and human, clothing and identity, and with its playful mobilization of homonyms, to the essentially flat world in which a character like Lance lives? Lear's transformation into an animal-made object resonates with Lance's staged complaint because he too fails to find compassion in his 'centaur' daughters. But the lower-class Lance generates different audience expectations and a different place in his 'world'. Like Bottom, that other hybrid 'mechanical', Lance is already more dehumanized, more object-like than anyone in *Lear*. Dare I point out the echoes also of Lavinia's vegetative/meteorological state in Lance's sister's 'lily' whiteness or his mother's 'breath'? Or the stony cur Crab, who sheds no tears? And yet, this assemblage of entwined living and dead matter constitutes a family, indeed a moved and moving one. Posthuman Lance comfortably rejects Lear-like longing for an anthropocentric humanist cosmos: in his world, there is no need to ask 'Why should a dog, a horse, a rat have life / And thou no breath at all?' (*King Lear* 5.3.305–6). Shoes breathe, staffs moan and dogs have less life than stones. And all is well with the world.

5

Techno-Bard

In our previous consideration of animals as the vehicle for posthumanist readings of Shakespeare, we discovered that hybridity, initially fashioned by mixing human and animal, can also evolve into the interchangeability and interpenetrability of animals and plants. The entanglement of humans with non- or inhuman elements and objects extends equally to mineral matter. Titus laments his doomed sons, imagining that the stones on which he stands 'were they but attired in grave weeds' might make suitable tribunes for Rome (3.1.43). A moment later, discovering Lavinia's mutilation and Lucius's banishment, he becomes stranded on those stones: 'For now I stand as one upon a rock, / Environed with a wilderness of sea' (3.1.95). He addresses Lavinia: 'Shall thy good uncle, thy brother Lucius / And thou and I sit round about some fountain / Looking downwards to behold our cheeks. / How they are stained like meadows yet not dry, / With miry slime left on them by a flood?' (3.1.123–7). Titus's self-depiction migrates from weather itself ('O earth, I will befriend thee more with rain / That shall distill from these two ancient ruins'; 3.1.16–17), to meadow, to wet stone transformed by submersion in a flood. His psychic dislocation is expressed through these shifting, metamorphosing instantiations of matter, among which human embodiment is only one porous and beleaguered analogical option. Like Titus, rather than experiencing themselves as distinct from other objects and phenomena Shakespeare's human characters discover that they are enmeshed in an environmental web within which identity is constantly dissolved and dispersed.

Titus Andronicus is not the only place where we might find early moderns depicting environmental entanglements. The vegetable portraits of Giuseppe Arcimboldo render human faces through assemblages of organic matter, as if the human visage were merely a coagulation of non-human life forms. Robert N. Watson uses Arcimboldo's work to bolster his argument that *A Midsummer Night's Dream* deconstructs the bounded autonomous ego in favour of a 'permeable, ecosystematic self' (2011: 53), while art historian Pontus Hulten observes that the portraits are 'pantheistic', Ovidian and potentially egalitarian in that they represent great men via 'the leavings of the fruit and vegetable cart' (1987). Indeed, Arcimboldo presents art historians with a problem: the artist's very popular and abundant production of these images, some via commission by patrons like the Habsburg Rudolph II, the Holy Roman Emperor, for example (who is generally recognized in his image of Vertumnus – Figure 5.1), can't easily be assimilated to a narrative about Renaissance humanist ideals and achievements. Critics have often dismissed the portraits as 'bizarre inventions, capricci, scherzi'.[1] They are considered demonstrations of technical virtuosity but empty of larger meaning, except perhaps in their naturalizing allegories of monarchy and political leadership, or as assertions of the global inclusiveness of, for instance, Rudolph's leadership. Thomas DaCosta Kaufmann thus notes that their subsequent critical reception is 'unsettled', generating 'rival and contradictory' interpretations and assessments (2009: 7).

Yet for ecomaterialists these paintings can be fascinating in that they seem to concretize the idea of the human as not merely part of nature, but comprising its products, generated out of the copious explosion of flora and fauna (some of the portraits use animals) that is more commonly rendered in early modern art as separate from and under the control or dominion of human beings.[2] It is worth considering, however, that such arguments can run the risk of over-naturalizing

FIGURE 5.1 *Giuseppe Arcimboldo,* Vertumnus *(Emperor Rudolf II), 1590. Oil on wood, 70.5 × 57.5 cm. Courtesy of Art Resource.*

the portraits in turn, by overlooking or repressing those of Arcimboldo's works that do not involve natural objects, using instead human-manufactured or technological items to construct their 'human' images. For instance, in one, a librarian's head is composed of mountains of stacked books

(Figure 5.2); in another, a waiter's head is made up of the tools of his trade. Yet others involve the elements – earth, air, fire or water. In that series, animals provide the stuff

FIGURE 5.2 *Giuseppe Arcimboldo*, The Librarian, 1566. *Oil on canvas, 97 × 71 cm. Courtesy of Art Resource.*

of earth, air and water, but fire's visage is constructed out of burning fagots of wood, guns, cannon and 'fire strikers' (steel tools for generating sparks, and the Habsburg family symbol). In other words, human technology is as much on display in these portraits as is nature's bounty.

In this chapter, I follow up on this hint in Arcimboldo's work about the role technology plays in constructing versions of 'the human'. I turn to the diverse kinds and levels of relationships to human technology we find in Shakespeare's work to tease out their implications for individual characters, for play worlds, and also for the precepts of Renaissance humanism. Since technology looms large in current debates about what it means to be posthuman, and because technological change both supported and posed specific challenges to Renaissance humanist ideals, it is a significant domain in which posthumanist theory, history and early modern literature intersect. In the introduction I digested the work of N. Katherine Hayles, which found that both the liberal humanist subject and the cybernetic posthuman of the twentieth century involved the erasure of embodiment. Hayles resists that process, exposing 'what had to be elided, suppressed, and forgotten to make information lose its body' (1999: 13). More recently, in a retrospective on Donna Haraway's 1980 *Cyborg Manifesto*, Hayles proposes that we have entered a new frontier, what she calls the Regime of Computation. The internet, and all the networked and programmable systems that intersect with it, has extended computational models so that they might be said to constitute reality itself. Hayles embraces Haraway's insight into human co-evolution, observing that this new regime continues to involve a mutual and serial metamorphosis, with technological possibility shaping humanity and vice versa in a perpetual process: 'As inhabitants of globally interconnected networks, we are joined in a dynamic co-evolutionary spiral with intelligent machines as well as with the other biological species with whom we share the planet' (2006: 164).

What could early modern artefacts, whether Arcimboldo's paintings or Shakespeare's plays, demonstrate about such a 'dynamic coevolutionary spiral'? The Renaissance is partly defined by its rediscovery of classical knowledge, and its expansion of that knowledge through the embrace of new methodologies in nearly every area of culture, science, politics, economics, art and religion. Humans, however, as Hayles might point out, were not simply originators and masters of the various 'makings' involved – they were also in turn created and recreated through interactions with those methodologies and their material results. In their introduction to *Renaissance Posthumanism*, Joseph Campana and Scott Maisano argue that humanism was 'never a coherent or singular world view' but more a set of reading practices: 'Renaissance humanists demonstrated how close reading and careful restoration of ancient texts could be an effective means of situating and addressing ... the pressing philosophical problems of their day' (2016: 2). Just as human cognition is transformed in our historical moment through interaction with computerized information, which alters reading practices into hyper-reading or information-gathering practices (with possible consequences even for brain structure and development), so humanist reading practices were bolstered by, and inspired the invention of, new technologies that in turn changed how early modern reading and knowing happened. As Hayles notes, literary and artistic artefacts shape and disseminate the possible meanings of technological changes, and inspire the imagination of new forms or routes for technology (1999: 21).

Like twentieth- and twenty-first-century humans who are coping with the radical changes introduced by inventions like the internet, early moderns experienced a seismic shift in the speed and nature of knowledge transmission. The printing press, for example, was as revolutionary as the computer or internet, if much slower – and not just in social or political domains. Print seemed to promise a transformation of the very essence of human beings as well. As Leah Marcus points out, for instance, the possibility of creating a permanent memory through print 'c[ame] tantalizingly, heartbreakingly close to fulfilling the medieval and early modern dream of encyclopedic memory' (2000: 19). The explosion of printed matter meant that metaphors comparing human beings to books gained new dimensions of meaning, not to mention simply occurring more often. Juliet accuses Romeo of 'loving by the book' (*Romeo and Juliet* 1.5.110), a criticism that reflects the ubiquity of love poetry and its power to extend literary devices into the 'real' world of wooing. Likewise, Touchstone describes a 'quarrel in print by the book' (5.4.87) in *As You Like It*, in which he employs an understanding of the nuanced rules of engagement, rules that derive from models found in the explosion of conduct books read by aspiring gentlemen in the period. In this way, he derails a dispute altogether. Touchstone's comic turn requires a set of books that can be parodied, adapted creatively to a new use, and the result treated as if it were the very condition of all verbal conflicts.

Does Prospero's drowning of his books in *The Tempest* suggest that a human being like Prospero is somehow more 'human' when he gives up books, the source of his magical knowledge? Do his books dilute his humanity by giving him access to powers early moderns would have considered more proper to God?[3] Or do they corrupt him by allowing his 'human nature' to be eroded by a kind of *techne*, a capacity for making incommensurate with his place in the cosmos? In either case, the way the book and the human who seems to 'wield' it interact does not result in a clear or simple instrumentality of the book. *Hamlet* also portrays books as extensions of mind, in line with Marcus's observation. Hamlet vows to the ghost of his father 'from the table of my memory / I'll wipe away all trivial fond records, / All saws of books, all forms ... And thy commandment all alone shall live / Within the book and volume of my brain' (1.5.98–104). If books offer a permanent record that acts in lieu of memory, the mind and memory become in turn like books: as Gloucester says to Somerset in *1 Henry VI*, 'I'll note you in my book of memory / To scourge you for this apprehension' (2.4.101–2). We are so accustomed to the cliché that memory is like a book that we have lost track of the ways this version of extended mind took over and shaped our sense of the inevitable interpenetration of manufactured print and organic brain. For Craig Dionne, as we noted in Chapter 2, the reservoir of proverbs and adages that could be found in books offered suffering human beings a form of automata that provided both memory and history, and comfort in the very fact that they are the stuff of rote memorization.

Medieval and early modern fascination with automata, machines and invention has been the topic of recent scholarship in history, science studies and literary studies. What these accumulated investigations create is a kind of assemblage portrait, à la Arcimboldo, of a world in which humanism, and the human at the supposed centre of humanist thought, is under constant pressure from technologies of all kinds, a 'human' and humanism that threatens to become fully mechanical. As Jonathan Sawday observes, 'by the end of the seventeenth century, the dominance of the mechanistic model within European modes of understanding had become unassailable. The world, human society, the human and animal body, all could be analysed in terms of the functioning of machinery' (2007: 190). Andy Clark has argued that transhumanist fantasies of human cyborgs miss a crucial point: that cyborgs are not merely formed through the union of human bodies with machines, but are the prior state of all human beings that makes such a union possible (2004). That is, for Clark all human beings are already cyborgian, a condition dictated by human adaptability to new tools and new technologies. As we saw in Chapter 3, there is no stable or 'real' division between mind and body, which means our minds are constantly engaged with and shaped by the environment in which we move and dwell. We reach into the world with tools, but through tools the world reaches back and reshapes us – our understanding of our environment, our functional expression of something we imagine to be the essence of our 'selves' is constantly under revision, under translation by whichever mode of interaction with the world we privilege at any given time.

Consider what some of our students might have to tell us about their experience of learning by rote. Every synonym for the word rote is mechanical in origin and import: if you're learning or acting by rote, you're drilling, grinding, on a treadmill, in a rut. The *OED* defines 'rote' as 'in a mechanical or repetitive manner: (*esp.* of learning, etc.) acquired by memorization without proper understanding or reflection'; but adds the now-obsolete meaning of 'with precision, by *heart*'. Rote practice, then, was once both mechanical *and* organic – it allowed for the indistinguishability of heart and mind, or heart and machine. Rote is also at the heart of at least one new and creative practice of reading in Renaissance England. In their discussion of Gabriel Harvey's marginal annotations, which we briefly touched on in Chapter 3, Anthony Grafton and Lisa Jardine propose a fascinating convergence of history, reading practices and technological innovation: they speculate that the only way Harvey could have kept the large number of books he was comparing at hand, yet have written within all their margins with such precision and clarity of penmanship, was to make use of a 'book wheel', a 'strikingly alien' device (1990: 46) invented in the period for just this kind of use. The wheel allowed numerous books to be laid flat side by side on shelves, but *rotated* on something that looked like the wheel of a watermill. It was, Grafton and Jardine argue,

> more than a device for neat storage of momentarily interesting texts. It belongs to Harvey's cultural moment, in which collation and parallel citation were an essential, constructive part of a particular kind of reading; it allowed the imbedding of text in context, after the fashion that Harvey and (we would argue) many of his professional academic contemporaries practised. The book-wheel and the centrifugal mode of reading it made possible amounted to an effective form of information retrieval – and that in a society where books were seen as offering powerful knowledge, and the reader who could focus the largest number of books on a problem would therefore appear to have the advantage. (48)

From the mechanized collation of classical texts Harvey was afforded by the book wheel to Prospero's drowned books, Renaissance knowledge flowed in and through objects that were organic and mechanical, and often both at once. Water, flax and animal skins made the book; goose and other bird feathers deposited the vegetable-based ink on their pages; the draft thus generated might then be reproduced by the movable plates of the printing press only to end up on a book wheel in the house of a nobleman, where a secretary like Harvey, who 'digested' multiple texts, could plumb them for insights on current affairs. Even learning 'by rote' (or rotation) thus involved, and still involves, a confluence of diverse factors, elements, processes and embodied beings. Humanism's reading practices turn out to involve posthumanist factors even in their earliest incarnations.

Leah Marcus's observation that printed books promised, but did not quite deliver, a permanent, complete and accurate version of memory indicates that our uneasy combination of reliance on, celebration of and suspicion of the internet is not new. Humans have always greeted technology's advances with conflicted emotions. Every technological advance comes with its disappointments and drawbacks. What technology like the printed book often seems to offer is complete supremacy over the recalcitrant body or mind, or over the non-human world – but never quite produces such complete domination, hinting at the self-deluding drive of anthropocentric thinking. Nor are technologies somehow distinct from and contingent on the prior existence of something called a 'human being': Clark is in many ways right that humans are coterminous with, defined by, and always already engaged in the use of technology; they are themselves always already inherently cyborgian. There are, however, specific technologies and specific relationships to technology that can erupt in ways that foreground this complicated relationship.

In what follows, I look at instances of imaginative engagements with technology that result in early signs of something we can call a Renaissance posthuman. I broadly interpret 'technology' loosely in this chapter to refer to all kinds of manufactured things, as well as the impulses and systems that allow those things to be created. In effect, I am using the origin term, *techne*, as my rubric, to allow for the diversity of ways technology was imagined in the period. I pay special attention to those kinds of inventions that were driving Renaissance art and science and challenging established pieties about the constitution of human identity. I begin with the charting of the human form in artistic representations, something very familiar to art historians and most students of the Renaissance. The advances – or more correctly, the recovered mathematical methods – that enabled more accurate representations of the human body also, I will argue, implicated that body in certain non-organic expressions of subjectivity. The drawings of Albrecht Dürer and Erhard Schön, which render bodies as stacked cubes, quasi-robotic figures composed of inorganic blocks, do not merely find a more successful way to depict bodies as three-dimensional solids in motion. They undermine notions of human integrity, unity and singularity. Technological knowledge in art thus radically re-draws the potential boundaries of the human.

I follow this initial set of observations with a reading of Shakespeare's history plays that focuses on a different kind of non-organic embodiment. This is accomplished via technology that bridges the apparent gaps between animals and machines, and between ancient and early modern culture, namely the iron-clad warrior knight. It might seem strange to call a knight an example of the period's technology, since by the time Shakespeare wrote, knights were obsolete, and even their Renaissance avatars, the mounted officer and the sword-wielding noble, were increasingly overshadowed by an actual technological advance, the creation of projectile weapons that used gunpowder. Although technology usually makes us think in terms of the future, even if it is a potential future in the present, Shakespeare's histories, where most of his 'knights' appear (some more knightly than others!) instead look backward to England's past. But there is nothing nostalgic about that backward gaze: Shakespeare at times makes the armour-clad body of the knight a figure for the degenerative amalgamation of human and non-human, and an emblem of human hubris. The knight's prosthetic extension of himself through his horse, the armour that he wears and the sword that he carries is acknowledged in the histories as the characteristic that defines knightly status, but the knight's capacity not uniformly cast as a celebration of human ingenuity, or as affirmation of human mastery over the self and the environment. Some military heroes are indeed noble, although even these can end up associated not with a central coherent ego, but with distributed identity. In other cases, the knight's trans-corporeal union with beast and metal is deployed in the plays to suggest that the whole concept of 'the human' is the territory on which violent conflicts are played out between forces and regimes of progress and change. Winners and losers are not neatly apportioned – in fact, over the arc of Shakespeare's two tetralogies, what constitutes 'modern' and 'ancient' becomes muddled, as do those who succeed and those who fail.

We should therefore take pains to avoid at the outset the pitfall of enforcing on Shakespeare's plays a teleological narrative of historical progress, with benighted classical and medieval sources unaware of and unaffected by human technological advances, superseded by the proto-modern Renaissance in which everyone was making new tools and thinking new thoughts (what Stephen Greenblatt (2011) has called the 'swerve' of the period). Such a narrative would simply fall in step with humanist and transhumanist fantasies about the eventual journey toward (transcendent, disembodied) perfection in humankind. Besides which, such a narrative would also simply be inaccurate, obscuring the ebbs, flows and cross-currents of interest in and application of technologies in Shakespeare's – as in every – era.

Blockheads and unravelled bodies

There are two things nearly every student of the Renaissance learns first about the period: that the rediscovery of ancient texts permitted the expansion of disciplines ranging from science to maths to literature to politics; and that the Renaissance celebrated the human in all its glory, decentring a biblically based study of God's word by focusing instead on all creation as the text of God's magnificence, and celebrating humankind's capacity to arrive at knowledge of God's works. One of the most famous and familiar examples of how these two innovations interconnect is found in Pico della Mirandola's *Oration on the Dignity of Man*, which tells us that God, the 'Mightiest Architect' (*Pater architectus Deus*) and 'divine Artificer' (*artifex*), placed human beings between the 'supercelestial region' and 'the fermenting dung-heap of the inferior world teeming with every form of animal life' (Pico della Mirandola 1956: 5) so that they might best comprehend and praise his works through the study of the liberal arts, that is of all past and contemporary knowledge:

> But upon man, at the moment of his creation, God bestowed seeds pregnant with all possibilities, the germs of every form of life. Whichever of these a man shall cultivate, the same will mature and bear fruit in him. If vegetative, he will become a plant; if sensual, he will become brutish; if rational, he will reveal himself a heavenly being; if intellectual, he will be an angel and the son of God. And if, dissatisfied with the lot of all creatures, he should recollect himself into the center of his own unity, he will there become one spirit with God, in the solitary darkness of the Father, Who is set above all things, himself transcend all creatures....
>
> In fact, however, the dignity of the liberal arts, which I am about to discuss, and their value to us is attested not only by the Mosaic and Christian mysteries but also by the theologies of the most ancient times. What else is to be understood by the stages through which the initiates must pass in the mysteries of the Greeks? These initiates, after being purified by the arts which we might call expiatory, moral philosophy and dialectic, were granted admission to the mysteries ... Let us be driven, O Fathers, by those

Socratic frenzies which lift us to such ecstasy that our intellects and our very selves are united to God ... For, raised to the most eminent height of theology, whence we shall be able to measure with the rod of indivisible eternity all things that are and that have been; and, grasping the primordial beauty of things, like the seers of Phoebus, we shall become the winged lovers of theology. And at last, smitten by the ineffable love as by a sting, and, like the Seraphim, filled with the godhead, we shall be, no longer ourselves, but the very One who made us. (1956: 8–9; 25–7)

The study of philosophy, Pico della Mirandola asserts, 'is what Moses beyond a doubt commands us, admonishing, urging and exhorting us to prepare ourselves, while we may, by means of philosophy, a road to future heavenly glory' (25). According to Pico della Mirandola, mankind achieves perfection and realizes God's plan in leaving him in control of his own destiny to rise or fall as he chooses ('cultivate' the seeds of his perfection and divinity) through the widest and most comprehensive scholarly curriculum that 'ask[s] the large[st] number of questions' (43).

For artists, a crucial part of that curriculum was the study of maths, particularly geometry, not merely to impose perspective on the visual field, but to more accurately represent human and other bodies, especially those in motion. One of the most celebrated and devoted students of the discipline was Albrecht Dürer, who published his *Treatise on Mensuration*, originally in German in 1525, translated into Latin in 1538, and followed it with *Four Books on Human Proportion* in 1528. Dürer's famous drawings of 'stereometric man' (a figure composed entirely of three-dimensional blocks) demonstrated the way the volume of human body parts could be represented visually in art through an assemblage of solids (Figure 5.3). These astonishingly de-humanized, deconstructed, quasi-mechanical 'human' figures are emulated in the work of Dürer's pupil Erhard Schön, whose graphed heads look like nothing so much as stacked blocks. Dürer's and Schön's blocky figures can be rotated to give a 360-degree perspective, allowing an 'omnivisual' or three-dimensional perspective. The result of these geometrical experiments, however, is a construct that departs dramatically from the organicism of other painted bodies in the period's art.

Granted that these studies are extreme renderings of a theoretical approach to the geometry of the human form, they have nonetheless attracted puzzled or dismissive reactions from some art historians. No less a critic than the influential twentieth-century scholar Erwin Panofsky observed that Dürer's fascination with geometry distracted the artist from his 'true' labour: 'Dürer ... succumbed, to a degree, to the temptation of pursuing the study of human proportions as an end in itself: by their very exactitude and complexity his investigations went more and more beyond the bounds of artistic usefulness, and finally lost almost all connection with artistic practice'. Panofsky calls Dürer's techniques 'cubistic', and the poses 'somewhat mechanical' (1955: 200).

> When Dürer, after the death of Maximillian I, felt free to devote more of his time to theoretical studies he took up his main problem, the rationalization of the human body, from a stereometrical instead of from a planimetrical point of view; and since the irregularly curved surfaces of a living organism are not accessible to elementary mathematical methods he tried to reduce them, as it were, to polyhedral shapes. (1955: 202)

Of one of the 'stereometric' figures, he writes: 'The various solids are shifted against one another like the parts of a mannequin; in fact one of these "cube-men" is combined with the sketch of an actual mannequin' (202). Yet Panofsky acknowledges that Dürer's figures can be 'strangely expressive', despite their 'preterorganic quality' (202). And these experiments are designed to allow 'the rationalization of movement'

FIGURE 5.3 *Albrecht Dürer, 'Stereometric Man'. Courtesy of the Saxon State and University Library, Dresden (SLUB Dresden / Digitale Sammlungen / S.B.6023).*

(202) – that is, to permit artists to capture in two dimensions the vital *mobility* of the organic human body.

Panofsky's fear that science somehow led away from art itself seems to resonate with contemporary Renaissance concerns that techniques like Dürer's stereometry, when applied to the human body, challenged previous, mainly religious conceptions of the human. Humanism, although often held in suspicion by religious authorities (and its defenders sometimes deemed heretics), justified itself through claims that it pursued knowledge about God through the study of his creation. That is certainly Pico della Mirandola's argument. Despite Panofsky's criticism, there was no assumed division between maths or geometry and art, nor as Pico della Mirandola signals, between science-based art and theological goals in the Renaissance. Leon Battista Alberti (the first Renaissance writer to discuss perspective at length) held that without geometry, painting cannot reach perfection; indeed, without geometry, painting's methods can't be understood at all, which leads to the failure of its goal, namely the recognition of nature's harmonious beauty.[4] Dürer declared that 'the measurements of the earth, the water, and the stars have become comprehensible because of the painted image' (quoted in Miles-Morillo 2010: 139). So the geometry of painting revealed the order of nature, which was in turn the means to know its creator. Yet the results, as Panofsky sensed, also demystified and despiritualized the embodied form at the root of art's versions of 'the human'. Schön's and Dürer's approach, while coextensive with Pico della Mirandola's humanist programme, turned sacred matter into a set of connected Euclidean solids, and thus into both a more fully knowable entity, and a less nobly contoured – and so perhaps less divine – one. In the words of Giancarlo Maiorino, Dürer's figures are 'cubic automatons', and as such are examples of a 'mannerist grotesque' (1991). Or, as Panofsky registers, there is something ultimately anti-organic about the method of representation that best permits the vitality of organisms to emerge in art.

Indeed, what Dürer's and Schön's stereometric figures reflect is a fundamental and often unrecognized paradox in early modern humanistic thought. For these artists, it is not merely that geometry overlays organic matter to make it more artistically manipulable, but that matter itself is revealed, through the study of disciplines like geometry, to derive its greatest vitality from the inorganic, abstract, inhuman laws of mathematics. The most lifelike, the most lively, the most natural painted body is one in motion; to manufacture its image requires that the fundamental matter from which the body is composed be conveyed via 'cubes', 'automatons', 'mannequins' and machines.

An extreme example of this intersection of technique and the object-status of the human body comes in a series of artistic *scherzi* related to Arcimboldo's composite visages (Figures 5.4 and 5.5). The work of Giovanni Battista Bracelli is not widely discussed in art-historical scholarship probably for the same reasons Arcimboldo's was for a time overlooked. Bracelli's *Bizzarie di Varie Figure* (1624) is full of human forms composed of different objects – many are merely hints of bodies created through unravelling strips or through stacked solids. It's difficult to reconcile Bracelli's oddly inanimate animated figures with the broader traditions in Renaissance art. Yet Bracelli deserves greater attention for the remarkable deconstruction his playful drawings enact on the human form. In fact, I would assert that Bracelli's images are not just jokes, playing on the use of inorganics to convey organicism, but rather that they propose that the 'human' is, for the purposes of artistic representation, essentially an assemblage of objects. What's more, at its heart the human is, if we take Bracelli's unravelling or outlined forms literally, *empty*, an absence, shrouded in layers of stuff that is not 'proper' to the flesh. Sometimes this stuff is ethereal, evoking the airy soul posited in religious doctrine; but often it is merely nuts and bolts. Like Dürer and Schön, Bracelli plays with blocks, the least organic form; unlike Dürer and Schön, his images are not teleologically driven by a desire for more natural representation. He is no geometer experimenting with movement. Bracelli's meditations on how we see and what we see oddly anticipate some of Descartes's most radical conclusions about other human beings in his *Method*: 'I do not fail to say that I see the men themselves ... and yet what do I see from the window beyond hats and cloaks that might cover artificial machines, whose motions might be determined by springs?' (1989: 84).

Dürer's stereometric man and Bracelli's unravelled bodies make the human coextensive with robots, androids and cyborgs. A number of scholars have begun to excavate the historical roots of such inhuman 'humans', physically realized versions of Dürer's volume studies and analogues of Bracelli's nuts-and-bolts figures. Jonathan Sawday, Wendy Hyman (2011), E. R. Truitt (2015) and Kevin LeGrandeur (2013) among many others have

FIGURE 5.4 *Giovanni Bracelli*, Bizarre Figures, *1624 (etching). The Israel Museum, Jerusalem, Israel. Vera & Arturo Schwarz Collection of Dada and Surrealist Art, courtesy of Bridgeman Images.*

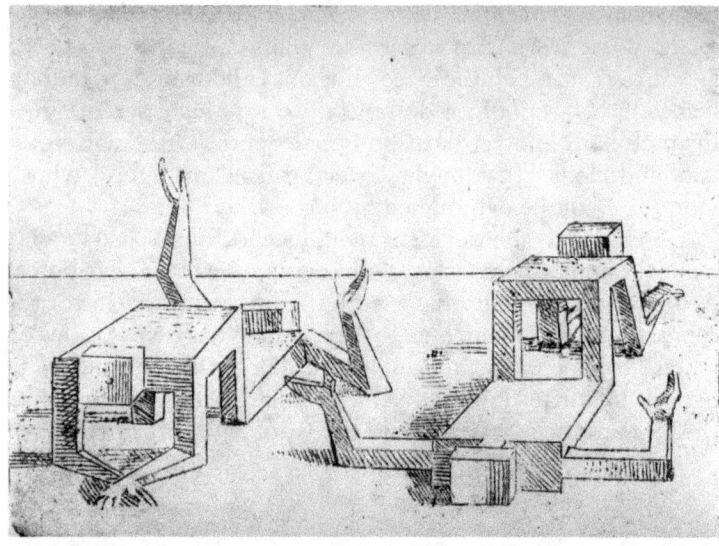

FIGURE 5.5 *Giovanni Bracelli*, Bizarre Figures, *1624 (etching). The Israel Museum, Jerusalem, Israel. Vera & Arturo Schwarz Collection of Dada and Surrealist Art, courtesy of Bridgeman Images.*

investigated early modern automata, and explored the questions that they about the nature of life itself, the distinction or lack of distinction between human and animal motion, and the means by which one can determine whether one encounters man or a machine. Sawday points out that machines have always been the uncanny doppelgänger of 'the human', with far-reaching consequences for philosophy as well as art (2007: 19). Whether the rise of technologies capable of creating automata are directly responsible for Descartes's perspective on the unreliability of the senses, for instance, or his creation of the 'beast-machine', is debatable. Yet there are clear resonances. Neil Badmington translates the extremely odd passage in Descartes's *Method* concerning a monkey that is potentially indistinguishable from an automaton as 'I think, therefore I cannot possibly be an automaton' (2003: 18), which he suggests is Descartes's more important impetus in writing the *Method* in the first place. Sawday sees instead an oscillation in Descartes's theory between biblical shame and divine consolation at the origin of Renaissance attitudes to technology, since the Fall introduces humanity to reliance on prostheses (the fig leaves, the city), but God confers the capacity to remedy the conditions of exile through 'human ingenuity and industry' (2007: 19). Descartes apprehends both dimensions of this oscillation, attempting to resolve it, Sawday argues, by dividing creation and withdrawing into the interiority of the rational mind.

A posthumanist reading of early modern art and philosophy like this one finds that something we call 'the human' does not precede technology and machinery, but rather that the human is already inhuman, that it is vital – mobile, animate, convincingly 'real' – because it is matter that follows rules of geometry in its animation. It exists, as Touchstone might say, 'by the book', because of the mathematical ordering of matter. But mechanical or cyborgian humans have a specific place in Shakespeare's works that narrows the field and involves other implications for both humans and humanism, as the next section will make clear.

Iron men

In *Titus Andronicus*, Tamora's son Chiron is an agent of discovery, a vehicle for confronting Titus with the instability of his identity. As Chapter 4 argued, Chiron's mythical origin invokes the centaur, both ideal and bestial, to complicate the assumption that human or animal might ever be fully distinct. Instead of being a special case, hybrids are the universal ground of creation. In part I insisted on this because we wouldn't normally expect to find a centaur in a play like *Titus Andronicus* – a tale about Rome, without clear heroes, enacted in the weary aftermath of war. That is not where centaurs, amalgams of noble humans and noble horses, usually appear. Instead, we might expect them to show up in Shakespeare's history plays, where actual noble warriors ride actual horses (insofar as theatre allows anything 'actual' at all).

The two most commonly cited examples of a human rider as centaur come from Sir Philip Sidney (in his *Defense of Poetry* and in the *Arcadia*, as noted in Chapter 4), aligning the centaur figure with chivalric and noble champions who win the day in battle atop their mounts, just as Sidney himself was renowned for doing.[5] And indeed we do get some of these in Shakespeare too – just not quite in the manner we anticipate. Centaur-like riders in *1 Henry IV* and *Henry V* turn out to be absurd throwbacks to medieval values and culture, characters who are least in control of themselves, and least capable of leading a winning army on the field (Watson 1983; Boehrer 2002; Raber 2016). Hotspur, whose name tells us exactly the nature of his shortcomings, and the Dauphin, who writes erotic love poems to his horse, will both be vanquished by Prince Hal, later Henry V. Hal himself is a rider who is so thoroughly encased in armour and so divine in nature that he fairly floats onto his horse, rather than mounting it like an actual embodied and earthbound human. His otherworldly equestrian skills impress Vernon:

> I saw young Harry with his beaver on,
> His cuisses on his thighs, gallantly armed,
> Rise from the ground like feathered Mercury,
> And vaulted with such ease into his seat,
> As if an angel dropped down from the clouds
> To turn and wind a fiery Pegasus
> And witch the world with noble horsemanship.
>
> (*1H4* 4.1.103–9)

I have argued elsewhere that this scene gives us not a true centaur (an animal-human hybrid), not even in the terms horsemanship treatises might have understood the concept, but a rider whose relationship with his horse makes him an abstract, mythic god manipulating a machine-like conveyance. Mimicking that debased relationship is Hal's relationship to his army in *Henry V* (Raber 2016). In that play his cavalry is composed of riders on 'poor jades', who 'Sit like fixed candlesticks' (4.2.45–6) on famished animals that

> Lob down their heads, dropping the hides and hips
> And in their pale dull mouths the gimmal bit
> Lies foul with chew'd grass, still and motionless.
> (4.2.47–50)

Henry V's triumph is not in becoming a better centaur than Hotspur or the absurdly horse-loving Dauphin, but in producing an army that functions like clockwork, surpassing human limits even if at the cost of both their and their mounts' vitality. Indeed, Henry's salient skill throughout the tetralogy is in transforming people into cogs in a machine – ultimately his brilliant machine of war – in order to defeat a much larger and better trained force. Drew Daniel observes of Henry's famous speech before the siege of Harfleur that it makes of the soldier's body 'a machine for replication and imitation' by a prince who 'samples' rhetorical materials much as would a hip hop artist, putting together 'in a collage the hardened and threatening aspect of war'. Harry's war machine 'disguises nature with the found materials of nature' to create a coherent historical narrative (Daniel 2011: 124). But between godlike Hal and his 'fixed candlesticks', between more-than-human monarchical subject and utilitarian object, lies an apparently unbridgeable gulf that makes Harry the master DJ in a world of vinyl discs.

Apparently is the key word here. Both terms in the analogy are emptied of the usual qualities that count as humanity, after all (Firestone 2014; Bertram, forthcoming). What is more, Shakespeare's history plays repeatedly provide us examples of human beings at both ends of the class spectrum who appear to function as machines. Most obvious are the noble characters who become 'themselves' most saliently on the battlefield when suited and armed with steel: in the words of the Chorus at the beginning of *Henry V*, 'Then should the warlike Harry, like himself, / Assume the port of Mars' (Pro.5–6). Throughout Shakespeare's history plays, audiences are thus introduced to examples of military technology, to familiar versions of human tool use involving the weapons of war; those weapons are then incorporated into human bodies and either made integrated extensions of the characters that wield them, or perceived as overwriting those characters entirely. Noble warriors may thus initially seem to be exemplars of human *techne* as a linear and one-directional (and class-based) orientation.

At the same time, the apotheoses of figures like Prince Hal involve human bodies that seem worryingly easy to turn into mere instruments. Randall Martin observes that Henry 'exhorts his soldiers to embrace this cyborgian metamorphosis' in *Henry V*, but then exerts a trace of caution, acknowledging that there is danger in turning men into 'brass cannon' (3.1.9–11; Martin 2015: 83). Falstaff, consummately and subversively sceptical of war's effect on men, presents Hal in *1 Henry IV* with a group of starved criminals at Shrewsbury, saying 'good enough to toss; food for powder, food for powder. They'll fill a pit as well as better' (4.2.64–6). Famously, Hal has no sustained objection to this characterization of soldiers as cannon fodder, nor will he balk at using his candlestick troops ruthlessly in *Henry V*. But Hal, like so many of Shakespeare's warriors, is himself not free from the reflexive definitional influence of weaponry. At his return to France after his great victory, Queen Isabel says she is 'glad to behold your eyes – / Your eyes, which hitherto have borne in them / The fatal balls of murdering basilisks' (5.2.14–17). Those 'balls' were Henry's monstrous artillery, which destroyed what Burgundy calls 'this best garden of the world, / Our fertile France' (5.2.36–7). Martin situates Burgundy's lengthy plea, which evokes nothing so much as dying Gloucester's vision of Edenic England in *1 Henry IV*, in his ecological analysis of the disruptions of new technologies for war: what was once the cyclical pattern of husbandry displaced and destroyed by war, followed by healing through the return to husbandry, erodes in the era of gunpowder.[6] Rather than a therapeutic balance, Martin argues that allusions to this georgic mode strike an elegiac note in Burgundy's speech. Henry's solution is to marry France to England by marrying the French princess. The play's final chorus lauds Henry: 'Fortune made his sword / By which the world's best garden he achieved' (5.Ep.6–7) – but then immediately calls attention to the significance of the past tense in these lines by reminding audiences that Henry's son would lose France in a series of military conflicts. Bertram uses the term 'perpetual war' for early moderns' experience of seemingly interminable conflict, while Martin accounts for the 'ecocidal' nature of artillery-based battles. Henry V, for all his investment in a fruitful marriage to repair the world he has damaged, will fail to restore a georgic peace for long. Instead, more 'balls' will fly to wound both France and England.

Timothy Francisco has argued of Marlowe's play *Tamburlaine* that it presents audiences with a mounted soldier who is essentially a cyborg, a combination of human, animal and metal; in a play that claims to 'bring a world of people to the field', Francisco notes that the playwright devotes far more time to animating with lush description their horses, rather than the men. For Francisco, Marlowe's play uses horses as a 'technology' of the battlefield that prosthetically enacts the penetrative bestiality of male martial subjectivity (2013: 47–8). Shakespeare's oeuvre includes some related, if less bloodthirsty, configurations of the warrior, both mounted and unmounted. In *2 Henry IV*, Prince John deplores York's appearance on the battlefield, surrounded by an army rather than worshippers appropriate to an archbishop, calling York an 'iron man' (4.2.8). York acknowledges 'The time misordered doth, in common sense, / Crowd us and crush us to this monstrous form' and names his army a 'Hydra son of war' (4.2.33–4; 38). The monstrosity of the armoured warrior pervades Shakespeare's histories, and a few tragedies, where men who wear iron are repeatedly translated into 'iron men', that is men without hearts, without conscience, and without, therefore, the stuff of humanity, whatever that might be. Martin points out that *Macbeth*'s initial picture of Duncan's thanes furiously attacking his foes as 'cannons overcharged with double cracks' is an ominous image, hinting at the carnage to come at the hands of 'martial cyborg' Macbeth (2015: 101). As Martin also notes, there is plenty in the play to support Roman Polanski's directorial interpretation of *Macbeth* in his 1971 film, which adds a last scene not in Shakespeare's play. In the film, after Macbeth's defeat and Malcolm's investiture Donalbain enters the witches' tent to restart the cycle of ambition, murder, war and ecological violence all over again. Polanski conjures perpetual war; like a rogue virus overwriting the ancient code of natural cycles, the transformation of men into machines of war cannot be contained.

In a rather more positive vein, Jeffrey Jerome Cohen observes that the medieval knight's body, which was itself understood to be a kind of *machina* or engine, was produced by an 'identity machine' that included his bond with his horse, his armour, the bodily requirements of 'hardening' for mounted warfare, and the complex and evolving culture of chivalry that positioned him socially, economically and politically (Cohen 2003). One small technological invention, the stirrup, made possible a vast set of cultural and material transformations: mounted knights could balance better, handle quicker movement, and so wield arms more effectively; horses were bred for more weight to accommodate the layers of mail and metal the knight then required, and so on. The result was a composite of animal, human and objects that together constitute what Cohen calls a 'chivalric assemblage', a 'network of meaning that decomposes human bodies and intercuts them with the inanimate, the inhuman' (2003: 71, 76). Both Francisco and Cohen insist that dismissing the language that constitutes such cyborgian identities as mere metaphor or personification is a mistake. The rhetoric reflects and constitutes material experience.

In much the same way that Chapter 3 found animal metaphor and metonymy becoming mobile and transitive in Shakespeare's plays, refusing to occupy stable points on a binary schema, we can find men and metal in the histories trading qualities and becoming mutually definitive. So, for instance, the iron shot projected by canon is, in *King John*, endowed with human outrage:

> These flags of France, that are advanced here
> Before the eye and prospect of your town,
> Have hither march'd to your endamagement:
> The cannons have their bowels full of wrath,
> And ready mounted are they to spit forth
> Their iron indignation 'gainst your walls.
>
> (2.1.207–12)

Talbot in *1 Henry VI* refers to 'quartering steel' as one of his 'attendants' (4.2.10–11) when he besieges Bordeaux, but finds himself surrounded instead by French troops. In turn, when his emissary, Lucy, entreats York for aid, he describes the army hemming Talbot in as 'a waist of iron' that 'girdles' him (4.3.21). Fifteenth-century knights wore a fauld and culet that created a kind of skirt around the waist and hips – a girdle, in other words, which is what Shakespeare plays on in the speech.[7] In Lucy's description, however, soldiers and armour are interchangeable, sharing more than a metaphoric connection, since both are generated out of the requirements of battle, and the identities of both are subsumed by the apparatus that is war.

Throughout the plays, descriptions of human temperament and will as 'metal' (often with the pun on 'mettle') or as specific kinds of metal like iron or brass, are common. Othello refers to himself as 'wrought' (5.2.345), the same term Cassius uses for Brutus's mind when considering whether he might join the conspiracy in *Julius Caesar* (1.2.308). Sometimes the metal involved is meant to resemble coinage, as in *Timon of Athens*, when Timon's servant remarks that Timon's friends have been found 'base metal' when they abandon him (3.3.8), or in *Measure for Measure* where Angelo asks for his 'metal' to be tested, only to enforce a draconian punishment on Claudio for 'false coinage' (1.1.49 and 2.4.45–6). But in those plays where military violence is at stake, references to metal or iron or adamant carry a particular weight. Talbot, for instance, scorns his French captors in *1 Henry VI*:

> In iron walls they deem'd me not secure;
> So great fear of my name 'mongst them was spread,
> That they supposed I could rend bars of steel,
> And spurn in pieces posts of adamant.
>
> (1.5.48–51)

The reason Talbot is so feared, of course, is that he is indeed a kind of 'Iron Man' (in the same sense as the current comic book and film hero of that name) – a fierce, almost godlike vehicle of noble rage, who wields his 'arms' with preternatural force.[8] It turns out, those arms consist of both his bodily appendages *and* his troops. When the Countess of Auvergne attempts to take him prisoner, Talbot scoffs at her efforts, claiming she only has his 'shadow', since his army, which stands outside her walls, is part of him:

> My substance is not here;
> For what you see is but the smallest part
> And least proportion of humanity.
> I tell you madam, were the whole frame here,
> It is of such a spacious lofty pitch
> Your roof were not sufficient to contain't.
>
> (2.2.50–5)

When the army makes itself known, Auvergne demurs: 'I find thou are no less than fame hath bruited, / And more than may be gathered by thy shape' (2.3.52–7; 69–70). Men at war are not simply human; they operate as extended, fortified beings, covered in armour and wielding weapons, supplemented by the soldiers they command.[9]

Bertram (forthcoming) takes account of the ways in which human, animal and inhuman materiel works as a vast assemblage in military manuals, where all are subordinated alike to the ordering of an army's ranks, practical needs and mobility. The Countess fails to solve his riddle until Talbot blows his horn and provokes 'a peal of ordinance'. At that point, his soldiers enter:

> How say you madam? Are you now persuaded
> That Talbot is but a shadow of himself?
> These are his substance, sinews, arms, and strength,
> With which he yoketh your rebellious necks,
> Razeth your cities, and subverts your towns,
> And in a moment makes them desolate.
>
> (2.2.60–5)

Like Arcimboldo's portraits, and with an echo of Bracelli's unravelled human figures, Talbot reveals himself to be a loose assemblage, a being made up of other human and non-human stuff. Rather than 'sinews, arms, and strength' residing in a fully realized embodied version of his self, he introduces his 'substance', the guns and troops he commands.

We could dismiss such moments as merely clever styling by a skilled playwright, involving merely the elaboration of figurative language appropriate to martial themes. But when cannon behave like human beings (with 'bowels' and 'wrath' and 'iron indignation'), when armies become iron straightjackets, when human characters show less emotion than does adamant, and when a character can claim 'the outward composition of his body' includes hundreds of serving men at arms, we must wonder whether the inert matter out of which armaments are manufactured doesn't also somehow contaminate the bodies, the minds and the environment of the people who use them. Erasmus thought so: in *Against War* he writes,

> But how much more grisly a sight is it, how much more outrageous and cruel, to behold man to fight with man, arrayed with so much armour, and with so many weapons? I beseech you, who would believe that they were men, if it were not because war is a thing so much in custom that no man marvelleth at it? Their eyes glow like fire, their faces be pale, their marching forth is like men in a fury, their voice

screeching and grunting, their cry and frenzied clamour; all is iron, their harness and weapons jingling and clattering, and the guns thundering. (1907: 15)[10]

Shaped by God first for friendship, with 'arms to embrace' his fellows, men gradually learned to kill wild beasts for protection, then for food; then through ingenuity and invention, to kill other human beings who seemed a threat, until mankind invented what Erasmus describes as the first military-industrial complex. War thus becomes 'common manslaughter and robbery', and migrates into perpetual war. Erasmus makes the case that, although ancient leaders like Alexander were 'mad', their wars were less destructive than those pursued by Christian princes: 'they were more faithful of their promise in war, nor they used not so mischievous engines in war, nor such crafts and subtleties, nor they warred not for so light causes as we Christian men do' (43). Erasmus offers a glimpse of the inhuman monster, fitted out with a carapace cobbled together from Nature's plenty, but unrecognizable to Nature herself:

> Yet behold thy self (if thou canst), thou furious warrior, and see if thou mayst by any means recover thyself again. From whence hast thou that threatening crest upon thy head? From whence hast thou that shining helmet? From whence are those iron horns? Whence cometh it, that thine elbows are so sharp and piked? Where hadst thou those scales? Where hadst thou those brazen teeth? Of whence are those hard plates? Whence are those deadly weapons? (16–17)

'Modern' advances in technology only alienate the warrior further from his 'humanity', emptying him of those things that to Erasmus signify human identity: 'But now this same thing is done more cruelly, with weapons envenomed, and with devilish engines. So that nowhere may be perceived any token of man' (15). For Erasmus, war, as Bertram observes, makes men who employ iron, and all the military hardware that term can encompass, into iron men.

Early modern warfare was so thoroughly changed by technology, particularly gunpowder and its various applications, that it would have been unrecognizable to medieval knights. Gunpowder had made the mounted knight of the middle ages obsolete – no shock force of mounted troops could withstand artillery fire. Yet Shakespeare's histories repeatedly return to the figure of the mounted warrior. Why? In the case of Talbot, the histories mark a loss; the hero of old is indeed admirable in his loyalty as well as his capacity for feats of arms. He is larger than life literally, since he encompasses multitudes. But he is doomed: Talbot dies because he relies on his peers, Somerset and Richard, who are more concerned with the competition for power and precedence, what Lucy calls 'worthless emulation' (4.4.21) than with serving England in war. Like Hotspur, Talbot is called 'overdaring ... unheedful, desperate, wild' (4.4.5–7); unlike Hotspur, whose rashness contrasts negatively with Prince Hal's patient Machiavellian scheming, Talbot's is lauded. And yet his fate in the play is not only to die, but to die with his valiant son, unable to overcome the consequence of his own reputation in teaching the young John discretion. As the son says, 'Is my name not Talbot, and am I your son, / And shall I fly' (4.5.12) when his father begs him to flee and live to continue the family name. A full three scenes are taken up with this pleading. The result: father and son die together. 'See where he [young Talbot] lies inhearsed in the arms / Of the most bloody nurser of his harms' (4.7.45–6) says Burgundy. At the last, Talbot is again other than a singular individuated identity, since he shares not only a name and martial aggression with his dead child, but a 'hearse' or coffin, where they both lie 'stinking and flyblown' (4.7.76). In the end, Talbot is not merely reduced from his status as 'great Alcides' to a rotting corpse but has lost the futurity that a male heir ensures.[11] In his loss of a son who bears his name, he is very like the elder Seward in *Macbeth*, whose stoic reception of the news of his son's death in battle confirms 'the nobility's lack of any serious alternative to Scotland's ecocidal polity' (Martin 2015: 104). While Talbot is marked as the embodiment of an obsolete commitment to the reproduction of iron men, Seward seems instead to signify the endless, almost robotic repetition of the same. But both share in the plays' profound suspicion of idealized cyborgian warriors.

Humanism's mechanisms

Thus far we have been employing a posthumanist repertoire to deconstruct 'the human' via Shakespeare's histories. But what about the human*ism* that informed the playwright's culture and perspectives and that we saw earlier generated the new military machinery through invention and the expansion of human knowledge? How might Shakespeare's military iron men raise questions about humanism's role in war, and war's role in defining humanism?

There is elsewhere in Renaissance literature an actual example of an 'iron man', one that Jessica Wolfe has argued represents an inherent tension not merely over what counts as human, but within humanism itself. She analyses the character Talus in Book V of Spenser's *Faerie Queene*, the squire to Sir Arthegall who enforces a justice that lacks the deliberative – and sometimes debilitating – mercy Arthegall is otherwise prone to. Talus is 'a mechanism designed to exact Justice without suffering from the infirmities of human feeling' (Wolfe 2004: 204). Although Arthegall has been trained by Astraea in 'all the depth of rightfull doom' that is justice (Spenser 1978: 728), he yet requires supplementation: thus,

> [Astraea] left her groome
> An yron man, which did on her attend
> Alwayes, to execute her stedfast doome,
> And willed him with *Artegall* to wend,
> And doe what euer thing he did intend.
> His name was *Talus*, made of yron mould,
> Immoueable, resistlesse, without end.

Who in his hand an yron flale did hould,
With which he thresht out falshood, and did truth vnfould.
(Spenser 1978: 730)

In the same way that Shakespeare's various depictions of the new technologies of war reflect anxiety over their consequences, Spenser is 'uneasy about these new methods of warfare and the virtues and social values associated with them' – but Wolfe adds to the mix a corresponding discomfort with 'human affection' exemplified in Arthegall, which compromises his ability to enforce justice (2004: 207). Splitting justice between human(e) Arthegall and inhuman (and often inhumane) Talus allows Spenser to more complexly interrogate the links between humanism and the prosecution of war.

Notable early modern humanists contributed to knowledge that made possible the new technologies of war, of course, but they also attempted to construct an idealized courtier who could either directly conduct successful military operations, or most effectively carry out a Prince's orders in battle. For every Erasmus who firmly decried the dehumanizing qualities of war, there was a Castiglione who integrated the achievements of an aspirational humanist education with military service, or a Machiavelli who provided the intellectual and philosophical basis for war.[12] Wolfe remarks that 'In the process of disclosing the incongruity of a militaristic neo-Stoic ethic when circumscribed by the larger mandates of Christian humanism, Spenser exposes the difficulties involved in the project of fashioning a virtuous man who is also a model soldier' (2004: 223). In his own consideration of early modern militarism and ecology, Bertram has instead argued that humanism itself produced continual war: in his view, the very anthropocentrism that informs Erasmus's anti-war screed, his celebration of the human as distinct from beasts who, unlike humans, cannot resist the brutality of their natures, leads to the first glimmers of what the twentieth century would call perpetual war. By reinforcing dichotomies between human and animal, Erasmus's positive exceptionalism, the product of his Christian humanism, enhances human beings' sense of disconnection from nature, which in turn can justify devaluing the environment being destroyed through war. The result is a loosening of the limits on war, and the discounting of its effects.

The Shakespearean iron men we have encountered here participate in the tensions, paradoxes and anxieties that both Wolfe and Bertram reveal in the work of other Renaissance writers. From Hotspur and Hal, to Talbot and Seward, Shakespeare's plays navigate the Scylla of noble militarism and the Charybdis of modern technologized war. The plays' cyborgian characters illustrate the temptations of humanism, its promise of mastery over other nature, over other kinds of humans; the lure of singularity, nobility and distinction; and the privileging of 'the human' as a transcendent being, moving ineluctably toward a more perfectly 'modern' technologically advanced state of being. But, as the work of Arcimboldo, Dürer and Bracelli might remind us, these constructions are illusions.

6

Post-posthumanism? Back to the Future

Renaissance humanism, more internally conflicted and complex than its reconstructions in posthumanist theory might allow, nevertheless helped accelerate a cultural shift, the consequences of which involved the reordering of education, politics, religion and many other aspects of life. While it is perhaps impossible to simply assert that humanism located the human (recalling Latour's formulation with which I began this book), it undoubtedly puzzled over a spectrum of articulations of that creature's nature. Posthumanism may well represent – certainly it aspires to represent – another such historical event, a sweeping philosophical and cultural reorientation. Ecological damage has put the planet in danger; species are disappearing at an accelerating rate; technology is transforming human bodies and minds, restructuring our social and material environments. Posthumanism positions itself as an intervention in these developments, reintroducing a more rigorous scepticism about the anthropocentrism that has allowed such things to come to pass, and hoping to increase awareness of human 'finitude and dependency' (Wolfe 2010: xvi). It is tempting to see ourselves repeating the seismic upheavals of the past, making possible a new appreciation of our entanglement in matter and of the vulnerability we share with other animals and forms of life, and perhaps endowing humanity with a humility we find appallingly absent in the past.

In my introduction, I cautioned against imposing a utopian teleological narrative on the development or the goals of posthumanism. Along the way, and for related reasons, I noted the problems with Stephen Greenblatt's idea that the Renaissance was the moment of a 'swerve' toward modernity. Change happens; but our need to retrospectively find seismic shifts, turning points or historical pivots rather than the slow tectonic movement that those undergoing it would have experienced, overwrites history with our own need for a good story, the destination of which is our present and the future we want to believe we still have. Posthumanism has the potential to share in this kind of distortion, for example when it collapses Renaissance with Enlightenment humanisms, but also if it projects itself unreflectively into a past as distant and alien as the sixteenth and seventeenth centuries. In Campana and Maisano's estimation, there is a perhaps inescapable 'temporal paradox' involved in moving between posthuman and premodern (2016: 7), which is linked to the problem of using posthumanist theory to reinvent – and so secure – the future of the humanities. They reject the idea of 'fight[ing] anthropocentrism one close reading at a time' in favour of cultivating a 'transhistorical and transcultural conversation' (2016: 33). In the end, however, it is the past and future of 'the humanities' that is their objective. The theory validates and therefore recreates itself by projecting itself into both past and future, in a sense rewriting both the Renaissance and the discipline in which the Renaissance is now studied according to a specific institutionalized code; it is thus, to borrow a term from systems theory, *autopoietic*, self-making and self-sustaining. It is not yet always clear, however, how well posthumanist theory will interact with its environment, how successfully it will structurally couple with systems outside itself. Fighting anthropocentrism one close reading at a time is not a bad way to start testing its capacity: indeed, I'd suggest that we need a kind of 'slow posthumanism' that arises out of millions of cellular pulses across the strands of culture, the academy and individuals over a longer temporal arc. Such an objective is not incompatible with Campana and Maisano's, only distinct in that it knits the 'humanities' into a wider environment.

One strategy in thinking about what posthumanist theory can and can't do for either the present or the future might evolve out of our reading of *King Lear* in Chapter 2. What if, instead of privileging the play's charismatic megafauna like Cordelia, Edgar, Kent or Lear himself, we attend more carefully to the pitiable and foolish Gloucester who stumbles blindly, and feels and smells his way toward his end? His 'fall' off Dover cliff remedies his fallen state only through the intercession of his unrecognized heir, who 'save[s] him from despair' (*KL* 5.3.190) to allow him a more complex and conflicted death. What if instead of Lear, Gloucester is posthumanism's best model?[1] Posthumanism may or may not be the end of 'the human'. At best, what it may promise to give humanity is a limping journey toward a false death, temporary survival as a failing but still breathing shell of itself. Lear dies holding his daughter, agonized, looking still for life; Gloucester, forced by the loss of his eyes to introspect, dies 'smilingly' (5.3.197), hugging a tree. And it is his child, not Lear's, who soldiers on, who inherits the 'rack of this tough world' (5.3.313) that he must stoically bear without the option of a quick escape. Does this conclusion seem too limited? Too defeatist?[2] But imperial triumphalism, the besetting sin of 'the human', is precisely what the theory aims to undo. So, to summarize, I'm advocating a slow, disabled, but environmentally aware posthumanism that is wary of the minefields of Shakespearean, and Shakespeare criticism's, idealism, a posthumanism willing to relinquish things like life, love and family if that is what is needed.

Posthumanism has its own sins, depending on its particular theoretical expression: although Rosi Braidotti (2013) insists on posthumanism's importance for the rethinking of race, gender, class and ethnicity, some forms of posthumanist practice can obscure or overlook the operations of these social categories. Posthumanist ethics involves attending to the relations between ever more kinds of entities; in this it is a challenge to ethical traditions that rely on the human subject as the origin of decision-making and that thereby enforce an inevitable degree of exceptionalism. But, as Wolfe and others have pointed out, the human is never exactly done away with; it might well even be profitably made the object of even greater scrutiny. Are we then impossibly locked into self-referentiality? And is exceptionalism only a trap, or does it have positive uses in the world? Might we need both a strategic subjectivity and a strategic exceptionalism to put ethics into practice as politics or law? By looking backward, future posthumanists might arrive at more deeply grounded answers to such questions.

On a rather happier note, for scholars of Shakespeare and early modern literature and culture posthumanism has meant the profitable expansion of the archive. Forgotten texts, and previously overlooked elements of old texts circulate in new analyses. Each time I teach a course on animals in Shakespeare, my students experience the shock of recognizing that not a page of a play goes by without several animals or references to animals appearing, something they inevitably missed on their first, second and third readings before taking my class. The series of Arden Shakespeare Dictionaries now include alongside more familiar topics like witchcraft, women, religion, music, or politics and economics a thorough study of Shakespeare's plants and gardens, not for marginalized hobby-historians, but for mainstream use in building a new body of work on the topic. Meteorology, shipwreck, the lithic environment, geohumoralism, foods and eating practices, physical prostheses, farmyard relations – one can fashion a list of new areas of research and writing quite as idiosyncratic and unexpected as those Ian Bogost devises in his contribution to Object-Oriented Ontology, *Alien Phenomenology* (2012).

But as Derrida has warned, constituting an archive is both an act of political power, and an act of repression (1996; see also Wolfe 2010: 295). The digital nature of our new archives may only make these issues more acute – whose memory does the archive preserve? Which versions of 'human' are attenuated by digitization, and which will the new archivists promote by their choices? Again, looking backward can be useful. Stephanie Jed's *Chaste Thinking: The Rape of Lucrece and the Birth of Humanism* (1989) begins with the story of the author's 'accidental' encounter with a specific text in the archive addressing Lucrece's rape and subsequent suicide. Jed asks why this story is located as the founding myth of Roman nationhood – but that ends up being a question about both the materiality of literature and the trope of chastity Lucrece mobilizes:

> What is important to me in this investigation is how chaste thinking functions as a figure by means of which the linguistic materials representing Lucretia's rape and the materials of writing by which her story is transmitted can be related to the circumstances in which interpretation takes place and to the discriminations effected by interpretive practice. As a metacritical expression, chaste thinking refers not only to the rhetorical mechanisms by which the meaning of the rape of Lucretia is construed, but also to the material means by which her legend is transmitted and circulates in culture. (1989: 8)

The materials that constitute the archive of humanist documents, and thus the humanist tradition itself, are not, then, accidental; nor are they merely passive repositories for ideas. Archives are created objects that shape the kind of thinking that can be produced from them. What kind of chaste thinking does our current digital archive cultivate?

Some aspects of literature have yet to be thoroughly subjected to the tools of posthumanist theory. Campana and Maisano single out one of the essays in their collection for the manner in which it enacts systems theory to implicate form in its interpretation of Rabelais. By focusing on the 'silenic box' that accompanies the story of Gargantua's birth, Judith Roof illustrates disruptions that make the boundary and relation of inside to outside oscillate. In the estimation of Campana and Maisano, Roof's work does what Cary Wolfe turns to Niklas

Luhmann for in *What is Posthumanism?* (2010) – it gives us 'an object lesson' in how to entertain the complexities of 'self-referential autopoiesis' (Campana and Maisano 2016: 27). Let's be clear: Roof does not cite Luhmann at all, nor does she announce systems theory as her methodology. Rather, her reading of *Gargantua* finds the effects of that methodology already present in humanist discourse. For Roof, the abyssally enfolded silenic box described in conjunction with Gargantua's birth 'figures ... humanism as always a part of and boxed within something else; as the ever-delayed inside bound to an outside that presumably looks nothing like it, that looks like nothing human at all' (Roof 2016: 101).

In Bruce Clarke's *Posthuman Metamorphosis*, as we noted in Chapter 1, *A Midsummer Night's Dream* provides an ideal illustration of systems theory's concept of second-order observation, which makes visible or present the mechanism by which an object is being observed. In Shakespeare's play, two 'closed yet interpenetrating societies, human and fairy' are at work, allowing audiences to watch the ways in which these two groups observe each other (2008: 72). Clarke finds the play metamorphic when it turns 'the *transformation of observation* – as when fickle male lovers turn their erotic gaze from one female to the next' into the observation of transformation, which occurs when Oberon watches the lovers and Bottom under the influence of love-in-idleness (77). Roof and Clarke, however, are standouts at present because few posthumanist readings of Shakespeare's plays incorporate the insights of systems theory, or deal explicitly with literary form. Theatre seems (as Clarke's work hints) a natural fit, since the confusion of frames involved in the play-within-the-play and other self-referential techniques literally stages the paradoxical relation of object and environment. And theatre has been hospitable to readings of distributed and embodied cognition like those of Tribble (2011), Cook (2010) and Anderson (2015). The plays thus invite further investigation using systems theory, and further reflection on the importance of genre or the particular environments in which different modes are created and circulate.

Shakespeare won't save the planet; neither will he preserve threatened species, cure the oceans of pollution by plastics, end the exploitation of animals or of humans. Shakespeare didn't invent the human; 'he', whatever and whoever he was originally, has become a placeholder for all the things we want to believe make us exceptional – the poetry, the artistry, the trenchant social observation, the transgressive politics, the awareness of life and death that we find in the plays and poems. By making Shakespeare posthumanist are we simply repeating the apotheosis that has made him the exemplar of every philosophical and political position Western culture has adopted since the seventeenth century? Or are we using a valuable and powerful cultural instrument to transform our relationship to ourselves?[3] Can we, *should* we be decentring Shakespeare at the same time we are endeavouring to 'relocate' the human via our readings of his plays? When Shakespeare is merely one poet among many, when the plays circulate in a flattened landscape of all sorts of drama, what will we have gained, what lost? That seems a necessary, if perverse, question with which to conclude a book written for a series on Shakespeare and Theory. Or perhaps it is the most posthumanist question it is possible to pose.

APPENDIX

Podcast interviews with the authors of most of the titles in the *Arden Shakespeare and Theory* series are available. Details are listed below.

Available titles

Shakespeare and Cultural Materialist Theory, Christopher Marlow
http://blogs.surrey.ac.uk/shakespeare/2016/11/04/shakespeare-and-contemporary-theory-31-shakespeare-and-cultural-materialist-theory-with-christopher-marlow/

Shakespeare and Ecocritical Theory, Gabriel Egan
http://blogs.surrey.ac.uk/shakespeare/2016/05/20/shakespeare-and-contemporary-theory-24-shakespeare-and-ecocritical-theory-with-gabriel-egan/

Shakespeare and Ecofeminist Theory, Rebecca Laroche and Jennifer Munroe
http://blogs.surrey.ac.uk/shakespeare/2016/06/07/shakespeare-and-contemporary-theory-25-shakespeare-and-ecofeminist-theory-with-rebecca-laroche-and-jennifer-munroe/

Shakespeare and Economic Theory, David Hawkes
http://blogs.surrey.ac.uk/shakespeare/2016/05/05/shakespeare-and-contemporary-theory-22-shakespeare-and-economic-theory-with-david-hawkes/

Shakespeare and Feminist Theory, Marianne Novy
http://blogs.surrey.ac.uk/shakespeare/2016/05/13/shakespeare-and-contemporary-theory-23-shakespeare-and-feminist-theory-with-marianne-novy/

Shakespeare and New Historicist Theory, Neema Parvini
http://blogs.surrey.ac.uk/shakespeare/2016/08/29/shakespeare-and-contemporary-theory-27-shakespeare-and-new-historicist-theory-with-evelyn-gajowski-and-neema-parvini/

Shakespeare and Posthumanist Theory, Karen Raber
http://blogs.surrey.ac.uk/shakespeare/2016/09/30/shakespeare-and-contemporary-theory-28-shakespeare-and-posthumanist-theory-with-karen-raber/

Forthcoming titles

Shakespeare and Film Theory, Scott Hollifield
http://blogs.surrey.ac.uk/shakespeare/2016/10/28/shakespeare-and-contemporary-theory-30-shakespeare-and-film-theory-with-scott-hollifield/

Shakespeare and Postcolonial Theory, Jyotsna Singh
http://blogs.surrey.ac.uk/shakespeare/2016/07/19/shakespeare-and-contemporary-theory-26-shakespeare-and-postcolonial-theory-with-jyotsna-singh/

Shakespeare and Presentist Theory, Evelyn Gajowski
http://blogs.surrey.ac.uk/shakespeare/2016/04/29/shakespeare-and-contemporary-theory-21-the-arden-shakespeare-and-theory-series-with-evelyn-gajowski/

Shakespeare and Queer Theory, Melissa E. Sanchez
http://blogs.surrey.ac.uk/shakespeare/2016/10/18/shakespeare-and-contemporary-theory-29-shakespeare-and-queer-theory-with-melissa-e-sanchez/

Notes

Chapter 1

1. While anti-humanism can be part of posthumanism and the theory often overlaps (as I note later), I use 'anti-humanism' simply to refer to early criticism of humanism that may yet hold on to the idea of 'the human' or 'the subject' and thus is not yet fully theorized as a coherent anti-anthropocentric approach.
2. As Chapter 2 will discuss, the continuities between medieval and Renaissance thought features in A. O. Lovejoy's monumental early work, *The Great Chain of Being* (1936 and 1964), and has resurfaced in current scholarship to contest the idea of the Renaissance as either a radical break with medievalism, or even a founding moment for modernity. Indeed, it is worth noting that some of the most suggestive work on posthumanist theory and past literary periods is being done by medievalists (see Cohen 2003; Steel 2011). As an example of how the idea of the Renaissance as some kind of inherently different moment in history, see the hostile response to Stephen Greenblatt's 2011 *The Swerve: How the Renaissance Began*, which argues for a rather old fashioned narrative that has Renaissance rediscovery of classical texts liberating individuals from the oppressive weight of the Church, to think in new ways about the world and its pleasures. This book provoked widespread hostility from historians and literary scholars for its utter mischaracterization of the unenlightened Middle Ages. Indeed, the shift away from the use of the term 'Renaissance' for the period that encompasses everyone from da Vinci to Donne in the last forty years of scholarship testifies to the pitfalls of asserting distinctions among such periods of time, which are purely convenient fictions and never fully verifiable. As a result, I use the phrase 'early modern' and the term 'Renaissance' rather cavalierly in this project and without

intending to affirm something like a 'swerve' that occurs in this period.

3   See for instance http://criticalposthumanism.net for the theory's web presence; popular culture is also rife with references to the posthuman in science fiction (for instance, David Simpson has written an entire Post-Human novel series, while cyberpunk revolves around the nature of the posthuman).

4   Macpherson describes the 'possessive individualism' that shapes the otherwise divergent political theory of Locke and Hobbes (1962), namely the idea that an individual is proprietor of his own body, and that its labour belongs to him, to be sold or otherwise profited from on the market; Macpherson, a socialist, opposed this fundamentally selfish version of individualism.

5   Badmington (2003) cautions that apocalyptic accounts of the end of 'man' ignore humanism's 'capacity for regeneration and, quite literally, recapitulation' (11). It is this fact that makes Derrida for Badmington, as for Wolfe (2010) so important, since Derrida so insistently leverages humanist philosophy against itself, refusing the whole idea of an 'outside' to philosophy, yet using humanism's own mechanisms to undo its conclusions.

6   This sweeping set of generalities describes a shift from the establishment of quasi-governmental organizations like the RSPCA, ASPCA or the Humane Society (animals are a special kind of property requiring care), to the arguments for animal rights most often credited to Tom Regan (animals are not property at all, but require a degree of personhood under the law). In contrast, critical animal studies mounts a more broad and theoretical opposition to the very idea of a differential status for humans and animals based on something we call 'personhood' because it justifies exclusion and mistreatment in the first place. This is not a neat linear process, of course; the humane welfare organizations do not disappear, nor do rights advocates – indeed, in the case of the latter, more actual legal rights are slowly being awarded to certain animals. Yet the flaws in the grounds upon which those rights are awarded only becomes clearer as they are conferred, creating increasingly confusing category conflicts (are livestock the same as pets? Do wild animals have rights?). Something similar seems to be happening with other endangered non-humans: recently the Whanganui River was given legal status in New Zealand,

and movements are afoot to grant some animals, lab animals for instance, 'human' rights under the law. On the one hand, these developments might suggest that Latour's vision of a 'parliament of things' is in its first stages of coalescing; on the other hand, such events will almost certainly raise more problems over categories – why this river? Why these animals? Is it the human service or historical value that legitimizes their entry into rights? If so, 'the human' still operates to create divisions and marginalizations.

7 In this list, metametazoan refers to reproductive multiplicity; PWA refers to people with AIDS; and bodies-without-organs to Deleuze and Guattari.

8 Latour uses the term quasi-object (1993: 54) to describe things that are neither exactly natural nor exactly social, things that have agency and create relationships without being precisely alive or conscious subjects; hence, hybrids of subject and object, as in the case, for example, of money or a pencil or gender. In each case, the quasi-object defies binaries like real vs. social, or alive/dead, active/passive and so on, yet each 'circulate[s] in our hands and define[s] our social bond' (1993: 89) even though we have not necessarily 'made' them.

9 One could argue for including a fairly large number of other works here, but I am listing only the few that self-consciously foreground a posthumanist objective and methodologies.

10 It is important to note also that the idea that humanism, even Renaissance humanism, marks an initiating boundary for posthumanist theory is not accurate: medievalists like Karl Steel (2011) and Jeffrey Jerome Cohen (2003) productively employ the theory to informative ends. In fact, there is quite possibly no historical limit to the theory, since its target, the human, is always under construction, and therefore in need of deconstruction.

11 Those classical texts humanists were reading carefully included things like Lucretian atomism, for instance, which viewed all things human and otherwise as matter, or Pythagorean arguments for metempsychosis, which downgraded the supremacy of the human by claiming the soul could be reborn in the body of an animal.

Chapter 2

1. Lovejoy notes, however, that balancing the sense of the human realm as the sink of sin was its unique status as the nursery of rational beings: 'If it was the only region of corruption, it was also the only region of generation; here alone new souls were born, immortal destinies still hung in the balance, and, in some sense, the fulfillment of the design of the Creator himself was at stake' (1964: 103).
2. Lovejoy (1964: 108–110); he credits Giordano Bruno with the prior, thorough explication of this view of endless populated worlds.
3. Morton actually uses the term being-quake to describe the discovery of hyperobjects through new parameters of theory like OOO (2013: 19).
4. Fudge points out this moment as a (hoped) return to exceptionalism (2012: 56).
5. Stanley Cavell raises exactly the same question as he investigates the play's critical puzzles (1969: 28–182). Cavell's answer is simply that he is sent there 'by himself' and by Regan, and invents the cliff and suicide as a retroactive reason (282).
6. Most critics assume the earthquake mentioned by the nurse in *Romeo and Juliet* was the 1580 one: '"Tis since the earthquake now eleven years, / And she was weaned' (1.2.24–5).
7. Raleigh's letter, which Walmisley points out was probably written by Thomas Digges, can be found in Sheeres (1700); the quote is from Walmisley (1910: 528).
8. In 1531, Lisbon experience an earthquake and subsequent tsunami that resulted in tens of thousands of deaths; this and the earlier 1509 Constantinople quake and tsunami were well known, if not so thoroughly reported in print as the English 1580 event.
9. Gabriel Harvey's correspondence with Edmund Spenser about the earthquake appears in *Three Proper and Witty Familiar Letters* (1580).
10. Tarleton's poem appears in Fleming's pamphlet, transcribed into modern English in Campbell (1941).

11 This passage from the *Discours d'une merveilleuse et veritable copie du grand deluge* (1580, J. Coquerel, Paris) is translated in Haslett and Bryant (2008: 589–91).
12 I am grateful to my student Nathan Likert for suggesting and elaborating this connection in his own work.
13 See Shannon (2013: 88–100).
14 I'm using the formulation 'un-knowing' to reflect the unravelling of epistemological certainties, but also a divestment of epistemology full stop. Rather than having characters merely turn away from knowledge or deny it, I'm suggesting that the play puts the project of knowledge under erasure. In this sense, I'm qualifying Cavell's magisterial reading of the play which turns on Lear's desire to avoid recognition throughout – hence, Gloucester is the first person by whom he can tolerate recognition precisely because Gloucester is blind (1969: 279). Cavell's reading implicates readers and critics in the play's evasion or denial of knowledge (322); I am simply questioning, in line with Morton's theoretical position, whether the play endorses any epistemology that can be denied or evaded, in favour of a humbled and humbling ontology.
15 Mentz (2015: 23–4); the text has Kent remark on the 'rack of this tough world' (5.3.12) with a play on 'wrack' as in shipwreck.

Chapter 3

1 Farah Karim-Cooper discusses the particular significance of hands for early modern women in her analysis of *Titus Andronicus* as an 'amputation play' (2016: 57–61, 222), and notes that early modern writing on amputation showed an emerging sense of brain plasticity in adapting to prosthetic amendment (229–30). On Lavinia's silence and gender, see Gajowski (2007) and Munroe (2015).
2 On the pitfalls of 'speaking for' others, see Munroe (2015).
3 Disability's function in defining 'ability', which is otherwise a category with no content, is very like the way that animals

NOTES

4 construct the boundaries of what is human by demonstrating what the human is not.

4 Houston Wood and Lamb do agree about thinking disability in alternate terms to the tradition of defect and impairment, though Lamb allows disabled bodies to be both metaphor and physical things, while Wood might dispute the gesture of making disabled bodies other than themselves, overwriting their experience with literary tropes.

5 One can easily find a version of disability studies that wants to restore the disabled body to full humanity; however, recent theory in the field does not imagine such a recuperation of the various incarnations of 'humanity' perhaps understandably, given the inhumane nature of human and the problem of turning exclusion into inclusion at the cost of dismantling the very system that originated exclusionary definitions. See Wolfe (2010: 133–6); in tracing the many categories that are disenfranchised by the humanist self Wolfe follows Derrida, among others, in excavating the 'non-power at the heart of power' (2010: 95). The role of prosthetics in supplementing disabled bodies also complicates the posthuman/posthumanism distinction – one might have a cyborgian body and be a version of posthuman, yet that does not automatically challenge the pull of humanism in thinking about the cyborgian body. And while the category of 'the human' can have strategic political utility (see Goodley, Lawthorn and Runswick Cole 2014: 347), both 'the human' and 'ability' work similarly – each requires something against which to construct its boundaries, each is constantly shifting, requiring perpetual re-articulation to paper over its inherent instability. What is abled changes according to how a society experiences disability: at the point where the toll of an ageing population makes large numbers 'disabled' for instance, disability expands to include nearly everyone through the forced recognition of common bodily vulnerabilities. In a sense, then, we might say that both 'the human' and 'the able' are (productively?) disabled by this fluid non-identity, even as both exert constant discursive and material force.

6 See for instance, Bynum (2006).

7 Jane Bennett likewise discusses the interactions of food and bodily matter: in opposition to the 'conquest model' of eating,

she posits eating as 'an assemblage of human and non-human objects' that 'recorporealize in response to each other; both exercise formative power and both offer themselves as matter to be acted upon' (2010: 48–9).

8   Affect theory erases the distinction between mind and body in a related but distinct manner, bypassing the common association of emotion with 'mind', and instead locating it in the body's responses. The conscious nature of emotion and its origin in the immateriality of the mind has historically – at least for the last two centuries – been received wisdom; in anti-humanist theory, the frameworks through which emotion was experienced and interpreted were understood to be discursive, as much as material. Affect theory does not absolutely discount either, but is willing to accept 'the paradox that there is an incorporeal dimension of the body' (Massumi 2002: 5). Early modern representations of the emotions are particularly compatible with affect theory given the role of the humours and other material influences in determining what can be felt; for examples of this kind of work see Paster, Rowe and Floyd-Wilson (2004).

9   For analysis of the noisiness of both plays and the theatre, see Gross (2001).

10 Bottom's speech is the launching point for Mazzio's brilliant re-reading of early Protestantism's view of the body, which was neither so visually oriented nor so repressive of the senses as scholarship has often concluded (Mazzio 2009).

11 The deconstruction of the subject has been the work of decades of philosophy and theory. As Jean-Luc Nancy puts it, the subject is a 'principle rupture line' leading to the interrogation of 'interiority, of self-presence, of consciousness, of mastery, of the individual or collective property of an essence … the certitude of an authority and a value' (1991: 4); yet Nancy rejects the simple 'liquidation' of the subject (5), and asks 'who' comes after – not what, concluding that whatever this presence might be, it earns the name of 'freedom' (8). However plural, communal, and deconstructed this freedom is, it still seems to speak, or be spoken into being by, a quasi-humanist rhetoric, something Derrida engages with in his contribution to Nancy's collection (Derrida 1991).

12 The prefix *para* means both 'next to' and 'beyond'; it can refer to the monstrous quasi-human or the superhuman, both of which are fair descriptions of Lavinia (as I note, she lacks the usual means by which human status is secured; at the same time, she exerts the most profound power on the play – it is her mutilation, her suffering, that makes the denouement necessary). I use para-human to allude to discourses of disability, but also, because the term has a current pop-culture connection to the superheroes of graphic novels, games and other artefacts. All these subject positions have overlaps and coincidences, and thus tend to fray the 'human' supposedly at the core of creation.

13 There is of course a rich critical literature on the blush in Shakespeare undergirding readings like Swarbrick's: see, for instance, Iyengar (2005: 103–39).

14 On obligation and the prohibition on murder, see Levinas (1969: 201, 1985: 86). While for Levinas the face is not reducible to the features in any specific way, it oscillates between that and an abstraction that stands in for something other than the biological face and actual faces. This is why Levinas so often is questioned about what kinds of creatures can be said to have a 'face', as in the moment Derrida seizes on in his response (2008: 106–9). Whatever Levinas's face is, it is, however, always a human face.

15 Erica Fudge discusses the problem of faciality with regard to animals in early modern contexts (2013), finding that rather than perceiving their livestock as faceless undifferentiated herds, early modern husbandmen recognized individuals and engaged in face-to-face encounters with their animals, encounters that were mutual. In Fudge's view, the Levinas/Derrida debate is itself limiting for its failure to see any other history than the intellectual-philosophical one, which in turn blinds its participants to alternative histories (196).

16 It's frequently comical pop-culture version involves the faces we find in anything from a piece of toast to an electrical plug.

17 It is even possible Arcimboldo may have read and embraced da Vinci's advice, or stumbled across his own version of it: Kaufmann notes that Arcimboldo calls grotesque decorations *macchie*, or spots, the same word da Vinci uses in the quote above (2009; see also Maiorino 1991).

18 See Li et al. (2014); on the fact that pareidolia precedes conscious or intellectual processing, see Hadjikhani et al. (2009).
19 Studies have found that while some animals react to images that resemble facial characteristics of predators, this may or may not be the same as pareidolia in humans. Not surprisingly, given the relationship between pareidolia and pattern recognition generally, computers can be taught to experience pareidolia (Rosen 2012).

Chapter 4

1 Haraway announces 'I am not a posthumanist', claiming instead 'I am who I become with companion species, who and which make a mess out of categories in the making of kin and kind' (2008: 19). Yet Haraway's work, in its commitment to animals and in its philosophical allegiances (and even its disputes), is important to a posthumanist project.
2 In an Aristotelian schema, three kinds of soul existed: the vegetative, common to all living things, involving the maintenance of life via nutrition and the like; the sensitive, mainly possessed by animals that could move and interact with their environments; and the rational, possessed only by humans. Each type of soul was also possessed by the category above it in the hierarchy of creation, so humans had all three.
3 For a more complete review of the literature see Raber (2015b).
4 Haraway also has a problem with Derrida's tale about his encounter with his cat, whom she finds he failed to greet appropriately and instead turned into the stuff of philosophical reflection – exactly the opposite of what he intended (2008: 19–23).
5 Both Haraway (2008) and Latour (1993) argue it is, of course; I am merely taking the idea of 'nature-cultures' and the hybridity both observe in those supposedly 'pure' domains, and making the human-animal hybrid explicit *and* the direct topic of a reading of a literary example.
6 On the relationship between colonialism and language, especially as Caliban experiences it, see Stephen Greenblatt (2007: 22–51).

7	For a thorough exploration of how humans often fall into the category of 'asses', see Fudge (2006); on Bottom specifically, see Boehrer (2002: 44–6).
8	Shannon's point that this was not the main division; evidence of chaotic proliferation of kinds leads to more complex hybridities.
9	Shannon qualifies that the plays use other terms more common in the period to refer to animals themselves, terms like beast, fowl, etc.
10	A review of the criticism on Shakespeare and animals can be found in Raber (2015b).
11	Ian MacInnes (2003) argues that dogs were used to do similar work in identifying the national traits of England vs. France.
12	Bruce Boehrer offers a different perspective on hybridity and marriage: he argues of *A Midsummer Night's Dream* that marriage inevitably involves bestiality when women are imagined to be less than fully human (2002).
13	Brown (1998: 175). In addition to Brown's work on centaurs in Shakespeare, see Lawrence (1994).
14	Origin stories vary; some have Ixion raping the cloud-nymph Nephele, some have him lusting after Hera (the latter in Pindar). The centaurs themselves are either children of Ixion himself, or of the issue of the rape, his son, Centaurus, who mated with wild horses on Mount Pelion. What matters here is the rape at the heart of the tale.
15	He dies when pierced by one of Hercules's arrows poisoned with Hydra venom (again, sources give different versions of the tale); in constant pain, Chiron relinquishes his immortality to end his suffering, so ironically the healer is represented as unable to heal himself.
16	Demetrius's name is used in similar ways: while his name means 'follower of Demeter', the mother-goddess of the harvest, fertility and marriage, he repeatedly invokes the harvest to pervert its significance: 'first thresh the corn, then after burn the straw', he advises when Tamora would have Lavinia killed on the spot; 'this minion stood upon her chastity, / Upon her nuptial vow' (2.3.123–5). At the play's end, Marcus tries to restore the meaning of the harvest, and of Demeter's agency: 'Oh, let me teach you how to knit again / This scattered corn into one mutual sheaf, / These broken limbs again into one

body' (5.3.70–2), trading on Demeter's identification with cyclical rebirth. Then again, if Demetrius's mother, Tamora would thereby logically be identified as Demeter (for the goddess/follower relationship to make sense), the same perversions as we find in Chiron's name apply in a vegetative context. Tamora's name is also fascinating, since it likely derives from the biblical Tamar (Genesis 38) who, in order to secure her status in Judah's family when her husband and his eldest son Er dies, impersonates a prostitute to deceive Judah into having sex with her. When she becomes pregnant, she is accused of prostitution, but reveals her plot by presenting tokens Judah gave her in payment, thus presumably gaining status through the birth of Judah's sons.

17 Asclepius was Apollo's progeny, rescued from his mother's womb (or her funeral pyre, depending on your preferred source) by Chiron, who tended and then raised him.

18 Chiron and Demetrius exceed even the mutilation of Shakespeare's other origin myth, that of Philomela in Book VI of Ovid's *Metamorphoses*, whose tongue is cut out when she is raped by her sister Procne's husband, Tereus.

19 One exception is Dympna Callaghan's reading of *Venus and Adonis* (2003).

20 Such a conclusion is available in the work of many ecomaterialists; see for instance, Cohen (2015), Feerick and Nardizzi's collection (2012) or many of the essays collected in Eklund (2017).

21 For a similar reading of *Titus Andronicus*, but one focused entirely on the meaning of its cannibal 'medicines', see Noble (2011: 35–57). Noble observes that the play fails to establish a real distinction between civilization and barbarity, especially with respect to 'barbarous' Rome: 'Although the play depicts and attempt to remedy a body politic that is pathologically violent, in the end all of the sacrifices fail to result in a new social contract for Rome' (56).

22 The bit was invented by the Lapiths in most mythological accounts of the tribe.

23 When Shakespeare has Othello link the Anthropophagi to 'men whose heads / Do grow beneath their shoulders' (1.3.145–6), he may be conflating sources – the Blemmyes had facial features on their chests, while Pliny's account of the

Anthropophagi had them using scalps as napkins while they ate human flesh. Certainly either example emphasizes the out-of-placeness of humans as meat. Pliny references as people who drink out of skulls (so heads beneath shoulders), or may refer to other group of people altogether (Blemites).

Chapter 5

1. These terms are cited in Ferino-Pagden (2007: 15), reflecting early attitudes that saw the work as a series of jokes and comedic representations.
2. Arcimboldo's paintings are analysed in Watson (2006) and in forthcoming work from Vin Nardizzi.
3. Julian Yates (2015) and Steve Mentz (2015) both meditate on drowned books of various kinds.
4. 'I want the painter, as far as he is able, to be learned in all the liberal arts, but I wish him above all to have a good knowledge of geometry ... [no] principles of painting can be understood by those who are ignorant of geometry' (Alberti 1972: 88).
5. Sidney's career exploited the neo-chivalric fad at Elizabeth's court, but he also longed for a role in religious war, and when he finally got one, died like a hero on the battlefield.
6. The Virgilian georgic, written in the context of the Roman civil wars, posit peace as a result that requires constant cultivation – a process in fact, rather than a state of being. As Martin points out, the historical events of Julius Caesar and Antony and Cleopatra were the backdrop for the poet's work (2015: 20); for Virgil, peacetime agriculture is the 'ethically and ecologically superior state to war' (Martin 2015: 20) as expressed in the image of beating swords into ploughshares.
7. Since this innovation was new in the 1400s it was likely more of a commonplace for armies in Shakespeare's day than in Henry VI's.
8. Only Joan la Pucelle, divinely fortified, can defeat him, although she lets him live because God has told her his destiny is not to die at her hand; like all heroes and iron men, Talbot has a weakness, namely his son, and when his son is killed, he dies of grief.

9 Phyllis Rackin describes the conflict between Talbot and Joan of Arc in gendered terms, pointing out that 'His language reifies glory, while hers is the language of physical objects. The play defines their conflict as a contest between English *words* and French *things*' (1990: 150–1); however, I'm arguing that the 'thingness' of both warriors is an underlying ontological aspect of every warrior.

10 Erasmus's original title for his meditation on the evils of war in his *Adages* is *dulce bellum inexpertis*, a quote from Pindar, meaning 'war is sweet to those who have not experienced it'.

11 See Rackin (1990: 154) on the change Shakespeare makes to the chronicle histories in order to have Talbot and his son on field at same time; she reads the argument between them in much the same way I do here.

12 Castiglione asserts in *The Courtier* that the first duty of the courtier is war (1994: 42), but then proceeds to describe a host of non-military qualities he must also possess – both are part of the service the ideal courtier should provide; Machiavelli's *Art of War* brought the fruits of study of classical texts to military science, securing continuity between political philosophy and military science, although his privileging of Roman tactics and rejection of firearms would make his work less useful over time to his peers as a manual, rather than an articulation of principles.

Chapter 6

1 I'm indulging in something fairly commonplace here, surveying Shakespeare's plays and characters to see which ones serve up 'best practices' for posthumanist theory. For Dionne (2016), *King Lear* is the representative play, but Robert N. Watson looks to the comedies, especially *A Midsummer Night's Dream*, for their dismantling of the ego (2011), while others look to *The Tempest* (Mentz 2008) or *Hamlet* (along with *Lear*, the primary text for Herbrechter and Callus 2012a) as salient exemplars. The results of this game can be positive, reinvigorating or expanding the Shakespeare canon; but they also always lead to questions about why other plays

diminish in importance for a particular theory – why are *Titus Andronicus* or *Coriolanus*, for instance, so much more plastic to the theory than *Measure for Measure* or *Love's Labour's Lost*?

2   If we take Lee Edelman's interrogation of the child's role in securing futurity to heart, then perhaps Lear remains the preferable (queer) posthumanist model: for Edelman (2004), the tyranny of heterosexism extends to its celebration of an essentially narcissistic reproductive imperative (this, for instance, of the ever present injunction to 'save the planet' or a species or a natural resource for children, whose constant overproduction is precisely what threatens the planet/species/resource in the first place). Yet the rhetoric of futurity does seem especially faint in *King Lear*, especially in Edgar's last lines.

BIBLIOGRAPHY

Agamben, Giorgio. (2004), *The Open: Man and Animal*, trans. Kevin Attell, Stanford: Stanford University Press.

Ahmed, Sarah. (2006), *Queer Phenomenology: Orientations, Objects, Others*, Durham, NC: Duke University Press.

Alaimo, Stacy. (2010), *Bodily Natures: Science, Environment and the Material Self*, Bloomington: Indiana University Press.

Alberti, Leon Battista. (1972), *On Painting*, trans. Cecil Grayson, London and New York: Penguin Books.

Alkemeyer, Brian. (Forthcoming) 'Remembering the Elephant: Animal Reason before the Eighteenth Century', *PMLA*.

Anderson, Miranda. (2015), *The Renaissance Extended Mind*, New York: Palgrave.

Aristotle. (1962), *Meteorologica*, trans. H. D. P. Lee, Cambridge, MA: Harvard University Press, Vol. II. viii.

Bacon, Francis. (1996), 'The New Atlantis', in Brian Vickers, ed., *Francis Bacon*, Oxford: Oxford University Press, 457–89.

Badmington, Neil. (2000) 'Introduction', in Neil Badmington, ed., *Posthumanim*, New York: Palgrave.

Badmington, Neil. (2003), 'Theorizing Posthumanism', *Cultural Critique* 53 (Winter): 10–27.

Baumbach, Sibylle. (2008), *Shakespeare and the Art of Physiognomy*, Leicester: Troubadour Publishing.

Behar, Katherine. (2016), 'Facing Necrophilia, or "Botox Ethics"', in Katherine Behar, ed., *Object-Oriented Feminism*, Minneapolis: University of Minnesota Press, 123–43.

Bennett, Jane. (2010), *Vibrant Matter: A Political Ecology of Things*, Durham, NC: Duke University Press.

Bertram, Ben. (Forthcoming), *Bestial Oblivion: War and Ecology in Early Modern England*, New York: Routledge.

Boehrer, Bruce. (2002), *Shakespeare among the Animals: Nature and Society in the Drama of Early Modern England*, New York: Palgrave.

Boehrer, Bruce. (2010), *Animal Characters: Nonhuman Beings in Early Modern Literature*, Philadelphia: University of Pennsylvania Press.

Bogost, Ian. (2012), *Alien Phenomenology, or What It's Like to Be a Thing*, Minneapolis: University of Minnesota Press.

Borlik, Todd. (2011), *Ecocriticism and Early Modern English Literature: Green Pastures*, New York: Routledge.

Bozio, Andrew. (2015), 'Embodied Thought and the Perception of Place in *King Lear*', *SEL* 55:2 (Spring): 263–84.

Bradley, Andrew Cecil. (1904), *Shakespearean Tragedy*, New York, London, Bombay: Macmillan Company.

Braidotti, Rosi. (2013), *The Posthuman*, Cambridge: Polity Press.

Brown, Eric C. (1998) '"Many a Civil Monster": Shakespeare's Idea of the Centaur', *Shakespeare Survey* 51: 175–91.

Browne, Thomas. (1926), *'Religio Medici', 'Letter to a Friend', and 'Christian Morals'*, William A. Greenhill, ed., London: Macmillan.

Bryant, Levi R.(2011), *The Democracy of Objects*, Ann Arbor: Open Humanities Press.

Bulwer, John. (1644), *Chirologia, or the Natural Language of the Hand*, London: Thomas Harper.

Bynum, Caroline Walker. (2006), *Wonderful Blood: Theology and Practice in Late Medieval Northern Germany and Beyond*, Philadelphia: University of Pennsylvania Press.

Calarco, Mathew.(2008), *Zoographies: The Question of the Animal from Heidegger to Derrida*, New York: Columbia University Press.

Callaghan, Dympna. (2003), '(Un)Natural Loving: Swine, Pets and flowers in Venus and Adonis', in Philippa Berry and Margaret Trudeau-Clayton, eds, *Textures of Renaissance Knowledge*, Manchester: Manchester University Press, 58–78.

Campana, Joseph and Scott Maisano, eds. (2016), *Renaissance Posthumanism*, New York: Fordham University Press.

Campbell, Lily B. (1941), 'Richard Tarleton and the Earthquake of 1580', *Huntington Library Quarterly* 4:3: 293–301.

Castiglione, Baldassar. (1994), *The Book of the Courtier*, trans. Thomas Hoby, ed. Virginia Cox, London: Everyman.

Cavell, Stanley. (1969 and 2002), 'The Avoidance of Love', in *Must We Mean What We Say: A Book of Essays*, 2nd edn, Cambridge: Cambridge University Press, 267–356.

Churchyard, Thomas. (1580), *A Warning for the Wise*, London: John Allde and Nicholas Lyng.
Clark, Andy and David Chalmers. (1998) 'The Extended Mind', *Analysis* 58: 10–23.
Clark, Andy. (2004), *Natural Born Cyborgs*, Oxford: Oxford University Press.
Clarke, Bruce. (2008), *Posthuman Metamorphosis: Narrative and System*, New York: Fordham University Press.
Cohen, Jeffrey Jerome. (2003), *Medieval Identity Machines*, Minneapolis: Minnesota University Press.
Cohen, Jeffrey Jerome. (2015), *Stone: An Ecology of the Inhuman*, Minneapolis: University of Minnesota Press.
Cook, Amy. (2010), *Shakespearean Neuroplay: Reinvigorating the Study of Dramatic Texts and Performance through Cognitive Science*, New York: Palgrave.
Crooke, Helkiah. (1615), *Microcosmographia*, London: William Jaggard.
da Vinci, Leonardo. (1957), *The Notebooks*, abridged, trans. Edward McCurdy, New York: Modern Library.
Daniel, Drew. (2011), 'Scrambling Harry and Sampling Hal', in Madhavi Menon, ed., *Shakesqueer*, Durham, NC: Duke University Press, 121–9.
Davis, Lennard. (2002), *Bending over Backward: Disability, Dismodernism, and Other Difficult Positions*, New York: New York University Press.
Deleuze, Gilles and Felix Guattari. (1987), *A Thousand Plateaus: Capitalism and Schizophrenia*, trans. Brian Massumi, Minneapolis: University of Minnesota Press.
Dent, Anthony. (1987), *Horses in Shakespeare's England*, London: J.A. Allen.
Derrida, Jacques. (1991), '"Eating Well," or the Calculation of the Subject: An Interview with Jacques Derrida', in Eduardo Cadava, Peter Connor and Jean-Luc Nancy, eds, *Who Comes after the Subject*, New York: Routledge, 96–119.
Derrida, Jacques. (1996), *Archive Fever: A Freudian Impression*, trans. Eric Prenowitz, Chicago: University of Chicago Press.
Derrida, Jacques. (2008), *The Animal That Therefore I Am*, trans. David Wills, New York: Fordham University Press.
Descartes, René. (1989), *'Discourse on Method' and 'The Meditations'*, trans. John Veitch, New York: Prometheus Books.

Dionne, Craig. (2016), *Posthuman Lear*, Punctum Press.
Dolan, Frances E. (2014), *Twelfth Night: Language and Writing*, London and New York: Bloomsbury Arden Shakespeare.
Donne, John. (1959), *Devotions Upon Emergent Occasions*, Ann Arbor: University of Michigan Press.
Dugan, Holly. (2011), *The Ephemeral History of Perfume: Scent and Sense in Early Modern England*, Baltimore: Johns Hopkins University Press.
Dugan, Holly. (2013), '"To Bark with Judgment": Playing Baboon in Early Modern England', *Shakespeare Studies* 41: 77–93.
Edelman, Lee. (2004), *No Future: Queer Theory and the Death Drive*, Durham, NC: Duke University Press.
Egan, Gabriel. (2006), *Green Shakespeare: From Ecopolitics to Ecocriticism*, London and New York: Routledge.
Eklund, Hillary, ed. (2017), *Groundwork: English Renaissance Literature and Soil Science*, Pittsburgh, PN: Duquesne University Press.
Erasmus. (1907), *Erasmus Against War*, ed. Lewis Einstein, Boston: D. B. Updike.
Estok, Simon. (2007), 'Theory from the Fringes: Animals, Ecocriticism, Shakespeare', *Mosaic* 40:1: 61–78.
Feerick, Jean and Vin Nardizzi, eds. (2012), *The Indistinct Human in Renaissance Literature*, New York: Palgrave.
Ferino-Pagden, Sylvia, ed. (2007), *Arcimboldo: 1526–1593*, New York: Rizzoli International Publications, and Milan: Skira.
Firestone, Emma. (2014), 'Warmth and Affection in *1 Henry IV*: Why No One Likes Prince Hal', in Laurie Johnson, John Sutton and Evelyn Tribble, eds, *Embodied Cognition and Shakespeare's Theatre: The Early Modern Body-Mind*, London: Routledge.
Flaherty, Jennifer. (2011), '"Know Us by Our Horses": Equine Imagery in Shakespeare's Henriad', in Peter Edwards, Karl Enenkel and Elspeth Graham, eds, *The Horse as Cultural Icon: The Real and the Symbolic Horse is the Early Modern World*, Leiden: Brill: 307–25.
Francisco, Timothy. (2013), 'Marlowe's War Horses: Cyborgs, Soldiers, and Queer Companions', in Jennifer Feather and Catherine E. Thomas, eds, *Violent Masculinities: Male Aggression in Early Modern Texts and Culture*, New York: Palgrave, 47–65.
Fudge, Erica. (2000), *Perceiving Animals: Humans and Beasts in Early Modern English Culture*, New York: St. Martin's Press.

Fudge, Erica. (2002), 'A Left-Handed Blow: Writing the History of Animals', in Nigel Rothfels, ed., *Representing Animals*, Bloomington: Indiana University Press, 3–18.

Fudge, Erica. (2004), 'Saying Nothing but Concerning the Same: On Dominion, Purity, and Meat in Early Modern England', in Erica Fudge, ed., *Renaissance Beasts: Of Animals, Humans, and Other Wonderful Creatures*, Urbana: University of Illinois Press, 70–86.

Fudge, Erica. (2006), *Brutal Reasoning: Animals, Rationality and Humanity in Early Modern England*, Ithaca: Cornell University Press.

Fudge, Erica. (2008), 'The Dog is Himself: Humans, Animals, and Self-Control in The Two Gentlemen of Verona', in Laurie Maguire, ed., *How To Do Things with Shakespeare: New Approaches, New Essays*, Malden, MA: Blackwell, 185–209.

Fudge, Erica. (2012), 'Renaissance Animal Things', in Joanne B. Landis, Paula Lee and Paul Youngquist, ed., *Gorgeous Beasts: Animal Bodies in Historical Perspective*, State College: Pennsylvania State University Press, 41–56.

Fudge, Erica. (2013), 'The Animal Face in Early Modern England', *Theory, Culture, Society* 7–8: 177–98.

Fudge, Erica. (2016), 'Farmyard Choreographies in Early Modern England', in Joseph Campana and Scott Maisano, eds, *Renaissance Posthumanism*, New York: Fordham University Press, 145–66.

Gajowski, Evelyn. (2007) 'Lavinia as "Blank Page" & the Presence of Feminist Critical Practices', in Terence Hawkes and Hugh Grady, eds, *Presentist Shakespeares*, London and New York: Routledge, 121–40.

Gibson, William. (2003), *Pattern Recognition*, New York, London: Berkley.

Goldstein, David. (2013), *Eating and Ethics in Shakespeare's England*, Cambridge: Cambridge University Press.

Goldstein, David. (2015) 'Facing *King Lear*', in J. Knapp, ed., *Shakespeare and the Power of the Face*, Burlington, VT: Ashgate, 75–91.

Goodley, Dan, Rebecca Lawthom and Katherine Runswick Cole. (2014), 'Posthuman Disability Studies', *Subjectivity* 7: 342–61.

Gouwens, Kenneth. (2016), 'What Posthumanism Isn't: On Humanism and Human Exceptionalism in the Renaissance', in Joseph Campana and Scott Maisano, eds, *Renaissance Posthumanism*, New York: Fordham University Press, 37–63.

Grafton, Anthony and Lisa Jardine. (1990), 'Studied for Action: How Gabriel Harvey Read His Livy', *Past & Present* 129: November: 30–78.
Greenblatt, Stephen. (2007), *Learning to Curse: Essays in Early Modern Culture*, New York, Routledge.
Greenblatt, Stephen. (2011), *The Swerve: How the World Became Modern*, New York: W.W. Norton.
Gross, Kenneth. (2001), *Shakespeare's Noise*, Chicago: University of Chicago Press.
Grosz, Elizabeth. (1994), *Volatile Bodies: Toward a Corporeal Feminism*, Bloomington: Indiana University Press.
Hadjikhani, Nouchine, Kestutis Kveraga, Paulami Naik and Seppo P. Ahlfors. (2009), 'Early (N170) Activation of Face-Specific Cortex by Face-Like Objects', *Neuroreport* 20:4: 403–7.
Halberstam, Judith and Ira Livingston, eds. (1995), *Posthuman Bodies*, Bloomington: Indiana University Press.
Haraway, Donna. (1991), 'A Cyborg Manifesto: Science, Technology, and Socialist-Feminism in the Late Twentieth Century', in *Simians, Cyborgs and Women: The Reinvention of Nature*, New York: Routledge.
Haraway, Donna. (2003), *The Companion Species Manifesto: Dogs, People, and Significant Otherness*, Chicago: University of Chicago Press.
Haraway, Donna. (2008), *When Species Meet*, Minneapolis: University of Minnesota Press.
Harman, Graham. (2002), *Tool Being: Heidegger and the Metaphysics of Objects*, Chicago: Open Court Press.
Harris, Jonathan Gil. (1998), *Foreign Bodies and the Body Politic: Discourses of Social Pathology in Early Modern England*, Cambridge: Cambridge University Press.
Harris, Jonathan Gil. (2008), *Untimely Matter in the Age of Shakespeare*, Philadelphia: University of Pennsylvania Press.
Harvey, Gabriel. (1580), *Three Proper and Witty Familiar Letters*, London: H. Bynneman.
Haslett, Simon K. and Edward A. Bryant. (2008), 'Historic Tsunami in Britain since AD 1000: A Review', *Natural Hazards and Earth System Sciences* 8: 587–601.
Hassan, Ihab. (1977), 'Prometheus as Performer: Toward a Posthumanist Culture?', *The Georgia Review* 31:4: 830–50.
Hayles, N. Katherine. (1999), *How We Became Posthuman*, Chicago: University of Chicago Press.

Hayles, N. Katherine. (2006) 'Unfinished Work: From Cyborg to Cognisphere', *Theory, Culture, Society* 23: 159–63.
Henderson, Diana. (2010), 'Mind the Gaps: The Ear, the Eye, and the Senses of a Woman in *Much Ado About Nothing*', in Lowell Gallagher and Shankra Raman, eds, *Knowing Shakespeare: Senses, Embodiment and Cognition*, New York: Palgrave, 192–215.
Herbrechter, Stefan. (2012), 'A Passion so Strange, Outrageous, and so Variable": The Invention of the Inhuman in *The Merchant of Venice*', in Stefan Herbrechter and Ivan Callus, eds, *Posthumanist Shakespeares*, New York: Palgrave, 41–57.
Herbrechter, Stefan. (2013), *Posthumanism: A Critical Analysis*, New York: Bloomsbury.
Herbrechter, Stefan and Ivan Callus, eds. (2012), 'Introduction', in *Posthumanist Shakespeares*, New York: Palgrave.
Hillman, David. (2007), *Shakespeare's Entrails: Belief, Skepticism, and the Interior of the Body*, Basingstoke: Palgrave Macmillen.
Hobgood, Allison. (2009), 'Caesar Hath the Falling Sickness: The Legibility of Early Modern Disability in Shakespearean Drama', *Disability Studies Quarterly* 29:4 (Fall). Available at: http://www.dsq-sds.org/article/view/993/1184.
Hobgood, Allison and David Houston Wood. (2013), *Recovering Disability in Early Modern England*, Columbus: Ohio State University Press.
Höfele, Andreas. (2011), *Stage, Stake, and Scaffold: Humans and Animals in Shakespeare's Theater*, Oxford: Oxford University Press.
Hulten, Pontus. (1987), *The Arcimboldo Effect: Transformations of the Face from the Sixteenth to the Twentieth Century*, New York: Abbeville Press.
Hyman, Wendy Beth, ed. (2011), *The Automaton in English Renaissance Literature*, Burlington, VT: Ashgate Press.
Iyengar, Sujata. (2005), *Shades of Difference: Mythologies of Skin Color in Early Modern England*, Philadelphia: University of Pennsylvania Press.
Jed, Stephanie. (1989), *Chaste Thinking: The Rape of Lucretia and the Birth of Humanism*, Bloomington: Indiana University Press.
Karim-Cooper, Farah. (2016), *The Hand on the Shakespearean Stage: Gesture, Touch, and the Spectacle of Dismemberment*, London: Bloomsbury.
Kauffman, Thomas DaCosta. (2009), *Arcimboldo, Visual Jokes, and Still Life Painting*, Chicago: University of Chicago Press.

Knapp, James A., ed. (2015), *Shakespeare and the Power of the Face*, Burlington, VT: Ashgate.
Lakoff, George and Mark Johnson. (1999), *Philosophy in the Flesh: The Embodied Mind and Its Challenge to Western Thought*, New York: Basic Books.
Lamb, Caroline. (2010), 'Physical Trauma and (Adapt)ability in *Titus Andronicus*', *Critical Survey* 22:1: 41–57
Latour, Bruno. (1993), *We Have Never Been Modern*, trans. Catherine Porter, Cambridge, MA: Harvard University Press.
Latour, Bruno. (2005), *Reassembling the Social: An Introduction to Actor Network Theory*, Oxford: Oxford University Press.
Lawrence, Elizabeth Atwood. (1994), 'The Centaur: Its History and Meaning in Human Culture', *Journal of Popular Culture* 27:4 (Spring): 57–68.
Lawrence, Sean. (2015), 'The Two Faces of Othello', in J. Knapp, ed., *Shakespeare and the Power of the Face,* Burlington, VT: Ashgate, 61–74.
LeGrandeur, Kevin. (2013), *Androids and Intelligent Networks in Early Modern Literature and Culture*, New York: Routledge.
Levinas, Emmanuel. (1969), *Totality and Infinity: An Essay on Interiority*, trans. Alphonso Lingis, Pittsburg, PA: Duquesne University Press.
Levinas, Emmanuel. (1985), *Ethics and Infinity*, trans. Richard A. Cohen, Pittsburg, PA: Duquesne University Press.
Li, Jiangang Liu Jun, Lu Feng, Ling Li, Jie Tian and Kang Lee. (2014), 'Seeing Jesus in Toast: Neural and Behavioral Correlates of Face Pareidolia', *Cortex* 53: 60–77.
Lovejoy, Arthur O. (1936 and 1964), *The Great Chain of Being: A Study of the History of an Idea*, Cambridge, MA: Harvard University Press.
MacInnes, Ian. (2003), 'Mastiffs and Spaniels: Gender and Nation in the English Dog', *Textual Practice* 17: 21–40
Macpherson, Crawford B. (1962), *The Political Theory of Possessive Individualism, Hobbes to Locke*, London: Clarendon Press.
Maiorino, Giancarlo. (1991), *The Portrait of Eccentricity: Arcimboldo and the Mannerist Grotesque*, State College: Pennsylvania State University Press.
Marcus, Leah. (2000) 'The Silence of the Archive and the Noise of Cyberspace', in Neil Rhodes and Jonathan Sawday, eds, *The Renaissance Computer: Knowledge Technology in the First Age of Print*, New York: Routledge, 18–28.

Martin, Randall. (2015), *Shakespeare and Ecology*, Oxford: Oxford University Press.

Massumi, Brian. (2002), *Parables for the Virtual: Movement, Affect, Sensation*, Durham, NC: Duke University Press.

Maturana, Humberto R. and Francisco Varela. (1980), *Autopoiesis and Cognition: The Realization of the Living*, Dordrecht, Holland: D. Reidel Publishing.

Mazzio, Carla. (2003), 'Acting with Tact: Touch and Theater in the English Renaissance', in Elizabeth Harvey, ed., *Sensible Flesh: On Touch in Early Modern Culture*, Philadelphia: University of Pennsylvania, 159–86.

Mazzio, Carla. (2009), *The Inarticulate Renaissance: Language Trouble in An Age of Eloquence*, Philadelphia: University of Pennsylvania Press.

Meillassoux, Quentin. (2008), *After Finitude: An Essay on the Necessity of Contingency*, trans. Ray Brassier, New York: Continuum.

Mentz, Steve. (2008) 'Shipwreck and Ecology: Toward a Structural Theory of Shakespeare and Romance', *Shakespeare International Yearbook* 8: 165–79.

Mentz, Steve. (2012), 'After Sustainability', *PMLA* 127:3 (May): 586–92.

Mentz, Steve. (2015), *Shipwreck Modernity: Ecologies of Globalization, 1550–1719*, Minneapolis: University of Minnesota Press.

Mentz, Steve. (2016) 'Shakespeare without Nature', in Dympna Callaghan and Suzanne Gossett, eds, *Shakespeare in Our Time: A Shakespeare of America Association Collection,* London: Bloomsbury Arden Shakespeare.

Miles-Morillo, Lynne J. (2010), 'Composing a Self: Translation and Transformation in Durer's Humanism', *Prose Studies* 32:2 (August): 132–42.

Miller, Patricia. (1996), 'Jerome's Centaur: A Hyper-Icon of the Desert', *Journal of Early Christian Studies* 4:2 (Summer): 209–33.

Moeller, Hans-Georg. (2006), *Luhmann Explained: From Souls to Systems*, Chicago: Open Court Press.

More, Max. (2013) 'The Philosophy of Transhumanism', in Max More and Natasha Vita-More, eds, *The Transhumanist Reader*, Oxford: John Wiley & Sons.

Morton, Timothy. (2011), 'Sublime Objects', *Speculations* II: 207–27.

Morton, Timothy. (2013), *Hyperobjects: Philosophy and Ecology after the End of the World*, Minneapolis: University of Minnesota Press.

Moshenska, Joe. (2014), *Feeling Pleasures: The Sense of Touch in Early Modern England*, Oxford: Oxford University Press.

Munroe, Jennifer. (2015), 'Is it Really Ecocritical if I Isn't Feminist?: The Dangers of "Speaking for" in Ecological Studies and Shakespeare's *Titus Andronicus*', in Edward J. Geiswedt, Lynne Bruckner and J. Munroe, eds, *Ecological Approaches to Early Modern English Texts*, Burlington, VT: Ashgate, 37–47.

Murray, Daisy. (2017), *Twins in Early Modern English Drama and Shakespeare*, New York: Routledge.

Nancy, Jean-Luc. (1991), 'Introduction', in Eduardo Cadava, Peter Connor and Jean-Luc Nancy, eds, *Who Comes after the Subject*, New York: Routledge, 1–8.

Nardizzi, Vin. (2012), 'The Wooden Matter of Human Bodies: Prosthesis and Stump in *A Larum for London*', in Jean Feerick and Vin Nardizzi, eds, *The Indistinct Human in Renaissance Literature*, New York: Palgrave, 119–36.

Nardizzi, Vin. (2016), 'Disability Figures in Shakespeare', in Valerie Traub, ed., *The Oxford Handbook of Shakespeare and Embodiment*, Oxford: Oxford University Press, 455–67.

Noble, Louise. (2011), *Medical Cannibalism in Early Modern English Literature and Culture*, New York: Palgrave Macmillan.

Panofsky, Erwin. (1955), *The Life and Art of Albrecht Durer*, Princeton: Princeton University Press.

Paster, Gail Kern. (1993), *The Body Embarrassed: Drama and the Disciplines of Shame in Early Modern England*, Ithaca: Cornell University Press.

Paster, Gail Kern. (2009), 'The Pith and Marrow of Our Attribute: Dialogue of Skin and Skull in *Hamlet* and Holbein's *The Ambassadors*', *Textual Practice* 23:2: 247—65.

Paster, Gail Kern. (2016), 'Bodies without Borders in *Lear* and *Macbeth*', in Dympna Callaghan and Suzanne Gossett, eds, *Shakespeare in Our Time*, London: Bloomsbury Arden Shakespeare, 177–83.

Paster, Gail Kern, Katherine Rowe and Mary Floyd-Wilson. (2004), *Reading the Early Modern Passions: Essays in the Cultural History of Emotion*, Philadelphia: University of Pennsylvania Press.

Pfannebecker, Mareile. (2012), 'Cyborg Coriolanus/Monster Body Politic', in Stefan Herbrechter and Ivan Callus, eds, *Posthumanist Shakespeares*, New York: Palgrave, 114–32.

Pico della Mirandola, Giovanni. (1956), *Oration on the Dignity of Man*, trans. Robert Caponigri, Chicago: Henry Regnery Company.

Raber, Karen. (1998), '"Reasonable Creatures": William Cavendish and the Art of Dressage in Early Modern England', in Patricia Fumerton, ed., *Renaissance Culture and the Everyday*, Philadelphia: University of Pennsylvania Press, 42–66.

Raber, Karen. (2015a), *Animal Bodies, Renaissance Culture*, Philadelphia: University of Pennsylvania Press.

Raber, Karen. (2015b), 'Shakespeare and Animal Studies', *Literature Compass* (June): 286–98.

Raber, Karen. (2016), 'Equeer', in Valerie Traub, ed., *Oxford Handbook of Shakespeare and Embodiment*, Oxford: Oxford University Press.

Rackin, Phyllis. (1990), *Stages of History: Shakespeare's English Chronicles*, Ithaca: Cornell University Press.

Roof, Judith. (2016), 'Rabelais's Silenic Regime: The Fundamentals of *Gargantua*', in J. Campana and S. Maisano, eds, *Renaissance Posthumanism*, New York: Fordham University Press, 99–119.

Rosen, Rebecca J. (2012), 'Pareidolia: A Bizarre Bug of the Human Mind Emerges in Computers', *The Atlantic Monthly*, 7 August. Available at: https://www.theatlantic.com/technology/archive/2012/08/pareidolia-a-bizarre-bug-of-the-human-mind-emerges-in-computers/260760/.

Rowe, Katherine. (1997), '"God's handy worke": Divine Complicity and the Anatomist's Touch', in David Hillman and Carla Mazzio, eds, *The Body in Parts*, New York: Routledge, 285–309.

Sawday, Jonathan. (2007), *Engines of the Imagination: Renaissance Culture and the Rise of the Machine*, New York: Routledge.

Schmidt, Gary A. (2013), *Renaissance Hybrids: Culture and Genre in Early Modern England*, Farnham: Ashgate.

Schoenfeldt, Michael. (1999), *Bodies and Selves in Early Modern England: Physiology and Inwardness in Spenser, Shakespeare, Herbert, and Milton*, Cambridge: Cambridge University Press.

Scholtz, Bernard F. (1989), 'Ownerless Legs or Arms Stretching from the Sky: Notes on an Emblematic Motif', in Peter M. Daly, ed., *Andrea Alciato and the Emblem Tradition: Essays in Honor of Virginia Woods Callahan*, New York: AMS Press, 249–83.

Serres, Michel. (2007), *Parasite*, Minneapolis: University of Minnesota Press.
Shannon, Laurie. (2009), 'The Eight Animals in Shakespeare, or Before the Human', *PMLA* 124:2: 472–9.
Shannon, Laurie. (2011), 'Lear's Queer Cosmos', in Madhavi Menon, ed., *Shakesqueer: A Queer Companion to the Complete Works of Shakespeare*, Durham NC: Duke University Press, 171–78.
Shannon, Laurie. (2013), *The Accommodated Animal: Cosmopolity in Shakespearean Locales*, Chicago: University of Chicago Press.
Sheen, Erica. (2004), '"Why Should a Dog, a Horse, a Rat, Have Life, and Thou No Breath at all?": Shakespeare's Animations', in Erica Fudge, ed., *Renaissance Beasts: Of Animals, Humans, and Other Wonderful Creatures*, Chicago: University of Illinois Press, 87–100.
Sheeres, Henry. (1700), *A Discourse of Sea-Ports; Principally of the Port and Haven of Dover*, London.
Sidney, Philip. (1977), *The Countess of Pembroke's Arcadia*, ed. Maurice Evans, London: Penguin Books.
Siebers, Tobin. (2008), *Disability Theory*, Ann Arbor: University of Michigan Press.
Smith, Bruce R. (1999), *The Acoustic World of Early Modern England*. Chicago: University of Chicago Press.
Spenser, Edmund. (1978), *The Faerie Queene*, ed. Thomas P. Roche, Jr., New York and London: Penguin Books.
Statham, Rev. Samuel P. H. (1899), *The History of the Castle, Town, and Port of Dover*, London, New York, Bombay: Longmans, Green, and Co.
Steel, Karl. (2011), *How to Make a Human: Animals and Violence in the Middle Ages*, Columbus: Ohio State University Press.
Stewart, Douglas. (1977), 'Falstaff as Centaur', *Shakespeare Quarterly* 28:1 (Winter): 5–21.
Swarbrick, Steven. (2016), 'Shakespeare's Blush, or "the Animal" in Othello', *Exemplaria* 28:1, 70–85.
Thomas, Keith. (1983), *Man and the Natural World: Changing Attitudes in England 1500–1800*, London: Penguin Books.
Tillyard, Eustace M. W. (1961), *The Elizabethan World Picture*, New York: Vintage Books.
Titus. (1999) [Film], Dir. Julie Taymor, Fox Searchlight Pictures.
Totaro, Rebecca. (Forthcoming), *Meteorology and Physiology in Early Modern Culture: Earthquakes, Human Identity, and Textual Representation*, New York: Routledge.

Tribble, Evelyn. (2011), *Cognition in the Globe: Attention and Memory in Shakespeare's Theater*, New York: Palgrave.
Truitt, Elly R. (2015), *Medieval Robots: Mechanism, Magic, Nature, and Art*, Philadelphia: University of Pennsylvania Press.
Turner, Henry. (1997) 'King Lear Without: The Heath', *Renaissance Drama* 28: 161–93.
Varela, Francisco, Evan Thompson and Eleanor Rosch. (1991), *The Embodied Mind: Cognitive Science and Human Experience*, Cambridge, MA: MIT Press.
Vesalius, Andreas. (1999), *De Humani Corporis Fabrica*, trans. William Frank Richardson, in collaboration with John Burd Carman, San Francisco: Norman Publishing, 2 vols.
Walmisley, Arthur. (1910), 'The Port of Dover', *Journal of the Royal Society of Arts* 58 (15 April): 526–38.
Watson, Robert N. (1983), 'Horsemanship in Shakespeare's Second Tetralogy', *English Literary Renaissance* 13:3: 274–300.
Watson, Robert N. (2006), *Back to Nature: The Green and the Real in the Late Renaissance*, Philadelphia: University of Pennsylvania Press.
Watson, Robert N. (2011), 'The Ecology of Self in Midsummer Night's Dream', in Lynne Bruckner and Dan Brayton, eds, *Ecocritical Shakespeare*, Burlington, VT: Ashgate, 33–56.
Wolfe, Cary. (2003), *Animal Rites: American Culture, the Discourse of Species, and Posthumanist Theory*, Chicago: University of Chicago Press.
Wolfe, Cary. (2010), *What is Posthumanism?* Minneapolis: University of Minnesota Press.
Wolfe, Jessica. (2004), *Humanism, Machinery, and Renaissance Literature*, Cambridge: Cambridge University Press.
Wood, David Houston. (2016), 'Shakespeare and Variant Embodiment', in Dympna Callaghan and Suzanne Gossett, eds, *Shakespeare in Our Time: A Shakespeare Association of American Collection*, London: Bloomsbury Arden Shakespeare.
Yates, James. (1582), *The Castell of Courtesy*, London.
Yates, Julian. (2015), 'Wet?' in Jeffrey Jerome Cohen and Lowell Duckert, eds, *Elemental Ecocriticism: Thinking with Earth, Air Water, and Fire*, Minneapolis: University of Minnesota Press, 183–208.

INDEX

Actor-Network Theory (ANT), 14
affect theory, 174 n.8
Agamben, Giorgio, 94, 105
Ahmed, Sarah, 41
Alaimo, Stacy, 17, 64
Alberti, Leon Battista, 141
Alkemeyer, Brian, 116
Anderson, Miranda, 72
animal rights, 169–70 n.6
animal studies, 12–14
animals in theory, 89–95
Anthropocene, 12–13
Arcimboldo, Giuseppe, 126–9
Aristotle, 176 n.2

Bacon, Francis, 30
Badmington, Neil, 144–5, 169 n.5
Baumbach, Sibylle, 75
Becon, Thomas, 110
Behar, Katherine, 79–80, 87
Bennett, Jane, 14, 173–4 n.7
Bertram, Benjamin, 23, 149, 152, 154, 157
body, 16–17, 56–8. *See also* face
   body/mind dualism, 58
   disabled/able, 55–6, 59–68, 173 n.5
   Enlightenment concept of, 16
   hands, 110–12
   humoral, 59, 63
   senses, 65–8
   and technology, 135, 138–56
Boehrer, Bruce, 92, 99, 107, 177 n.12
Bogost, Ian, 162
Bracelli, Giovanni Battista, 142–5
Bradley, A. C., 38–9, 42
Braidotti, Rosi, 3, 4, 161
Brown, Eric, 105, 108
Browne, Thomas, 118–19
Bulwer, John, 111

Calarco, Matthew, 94
Campana, Joseph and Scott Maisano, 5, 20–1, 22, 130, 160, 163
Castiglione, Baldassare, 180 n.12
Cavell, Stanley, 171 n.5, 172 n.14
centaurs, 104–15, 116, 146, 175 n.14. *See also* Chiron
Chiron, 107–15, 145, 177 n.15
Clark, Andy and David Chalmers, 70, 71
Clark, Andy, 18, 132
Clarke, Bruce, 20, 164
cognition, 18, 164
   theories of, 68–74
Cohen, Jeffrey Jerome, 150, 170 n.10

INDEX

Cook, Amy, 71
cosmology, early modern, 27–9, 34–5

Da Vinci, Leonardo, 82
Daniel, Drew, 147
Davis, Lennard, 60
Deleuze, Gilles, and Felix Guattari, 78, 79, 93–4, 95
Demetrius, 177–8 n.16
Derrida, Jacques, 79, 92, 115, 162
Descartes, Renee, 9–10, 69, 91, 117, 143, 144–5
Dionne, Craig, 47, 132
Dolan, Frances, 66
Dover (England), 43
Dugan, Holly, 101
Dürer, Albrecht, 81, 138–42

earthquake of 1580, 44–6, 49–51
earthquakes, early modern theories about, 46–7
ecocriticism, 12
Edelman, Lee, 181 n.2
Egan, Gabriel, 31
Erasmus, Desiderius, 153–4
Estok, Simon, 120

face, 61–2, 74–87
Feerick, Jean and Vin Nardizzi, 20
Francisco, Timothy, 149
Freud, Sigmund, 11, 69
Fudge, Erica, 23, 90, 99, 102–3, 119–20, 120–1, 175 n.15

Gaia Hypothesis, 31–2, 35
georgic, 179 n.6
Gibson, William, 83

Goldstein, David, 75, 79, 119
Gouwens, Kenneth, 21–2
Greenblatt, Stephen, 168 n.2, 176 n.6

Haraway, Donna, 89–90, 93, 129, 176 n.1, 176 n.4
Harris, Jonathan Gil, 66
Hassan, Ihab, 3
Hayles, N. Katherine, 6–9, 58, 129, 130
Herbrechter, Stephan and Ivan Callus, 20, 22, 23
Hillman, David, 64
Höfele, Andreas, 91
horsemanship, 136, 146–7. *See also* centaur
humanism, 141, 159
  and the archive, 162–4
  and technology, 156–8
humanist education, 138
hybrid, human-animal, 95–9, 103–4, 109
hyperobjects, 36–8, 42, 49–50

Jed, Stephanie, 163

Kant, Immanuel, 10, 69
Karim-Cooper, Farah, 172 n.1
Kauffman, Thomas DaCosta, 126
Knapp, James, 75
Knight, mounted, 135

Lakoff, George, and Mark Johnson, 68, 70
Lamb, Caroline, 57
Latour, Bruno, 1–2, 4, 14, 24, 34, 89, 170 n.8. *See also* Actor-Network Theory (ANT)

Lawrence, Sean, 79
Levinas, Emmanuel, 79, 175 n.14
Lovejoy, A. O., 30, 34–5
Luhmann, Niklas, 18–19, 163–4

Machiavelli, 157, 180 n.12
Macpherson, C. B., 169 n.4
Maiorino, Giancarlo, 141
Mantegna, Andrea, 81–2
Marcus, Leah, 130–1, 134
Marlowe, Christopher, *Tamburlaine*, 149
Martin, Randall, 148–9, 150
Marx, Karl, 5, 11, 69
Massumi, Brian, 16–17
Maturana, Humberto, and Francisco Varela, 68
Mentz, Steve, 32–3, 44, 48, 52
mind. *See* cognition
Morton, Timothy, 36–8, 39. *See also* hyperobjects
Munroe, Jennifer, 74

Nancy, Jean-Luc, 174 n.11
Nardizzi, Vin, 56–7
new materialism, 14–16, 117. *See also* Actor-Network Theory (ANT); Object-Oriented Ontology (OOO)
Noble, Louise, 178 n.21

Object-Oriented Ontology (OOO), 14
Ovid, 178 n.18

Panofsky, Erwin, 139–40
pareidolia, 62, 80–4. *See also* cognition

Paster, Gail Kern, 63–4, 75–6
Pico della Mirandola, 30, 137–8, 141
Polanski, Roman, 150
posthumanism, 159, 160
    definition of, 2–4
    distinct from the posthuman, 8
    and humanism, 3–5
    posthumanist ethics, 161–2
    relation to other theories, 5, 6–12, 159

Rackin, Phyllis, 180 n.9
Raleigh, Sir Walter, 43, 171 n.7
Roberts, Jeanne Addison, 103
Roof, Judith, 163–4
Rowe, Katherine, 111

Sawday, Jonathan, 132
Schmidt, Gary, 109–10
Schoenfeldt, Michael, 63–4
Scholtz, Bernard F., 112
Schön, Erhard, 128, 141–2
Serres, Michel, 118
Shakespeare, William
    and the archive, 23, 162–3
    plays:
        1 Henry IV, 28, 146, 148
        1 Henry VI, 107, 131, 148, 151, 152, 155
        2 Henry IV, 149
        3 Henry VI, 76, 77
        All's Well That Ends Well, 102
        Antony and Cleopatra, 28
        As You Like It, 77, 101, 131
        The Comedy of Errors, 78

INDEX

Coriolanus, 102
Hamlet, 23, 80–1, 131
Henry V, 107, 146–7, 148
Julius Caesar, 151
King John, 151
King Lear, 27–8, 37–54, 101, 161
Love's Labour's Lost, 84–7
A Lover's Complaint, 106–7
Macbeth, 48, 66–7, 119, 76, 149, 155
Measure for Measure, 151
The Merchant of Venice, 119
The Merry Wives of Windsor, 102
A Midsummer Night's Dream, 48, 67–8, 97–9, 100, 104, 164
Much Ado About Nothing, 67, 76, 103
Othello, 76–7, 105, 151, 178 n.23
Richard II, 28, 56, 101
Romeo and Juliet, 131, 171 n.6
The Tempest, 56, 97, 103, 131
Timon of Athens, 119, 151
Titus Andronicus, 55–7, 73–4, 107–15, 125–6, 145–6
Troilus and Cressida, 32–3, 56, 103
Twelfth Night, 28, 65–6, 78
Two Gentlemen of Verona, 99, 121–3
Two Noble Kinsmen, 101
The Winter's Tale, 77

Shannon, Laurie, 28, 41, 91
Sidney, Philip, 105–6, 146
Simpson, David, 169 n.3
Smith, Bruce R., 67
Spenser, Edmund, 156–7
Steel, Karl, 170 n.10
Swarbrick, Steven, 76–7
systems theory, 18–19, 160

Taymor, Julie, 55–6
technology. *See also* war
   automata, 132, 145–6
   cyborg, 132, 143, 149
   and the human, 129–56
   and humanism, 132–4
   'iron men', 135–6, 145–56
   print, 130
   stereometry in art, 139–41
Thomas, Keith, 91
Tillyard, E. M. W., 30–4
Totaro, Rebecca, 23
Tribble, Evelyn, 71
Turner, Henry S., 38–9

Vesalius, 111

war, 48–9, 153–4
   and the human, 157–8
   technology of, 147, 155
Watson, Robert N., 107, 126
Wolfe, Cary, 2–3, 25, 58, 96, 163
Wolfe, Jessica, 156
Wood, David Houston, 56

www.ingramcontent.com/pod-product-compliance
Lightning Source LLC
Chambersburg PA
CBHW050139240426
43673CB00043B/1728